MUSIC-HALL SERMONS.

BY

WILLIAM H. H. MURRAY,
PASTOR OF PARK STREET CHURCH, BOSTON.

BOSTON:
FIELDS, OSGOOD, & CO.
1870.

University Press: Welch, Bigelow, & Co.,
Cambridge.

PREFACE.

WITH the exception of a few verbal alterations, these discourses are now given to the public in the precise form in which they were delivered. Prepared as they were while the writer was under the pressure of continual duties, — in weariness often, and mid many distractions, — he is sensible of their literary imperfections. He laments most that the truths he aimed to inculcate suffer because of the weakness of the utterance.

W. H. H. M.

BOSTON, March, 1870.

CONTENTS.

SERMON VIII.

SERMON IX.

SERMON X.

SERMON XI.

SERMON XII.

SERMON I.

THE TENDERNESS OF GOD.

"A bruised reed shall He not break." — MATTHEW xii. 20.

THE world is hard, — hard in its policies, feelings, and acts. Its judgments are harsh, and its penalties are cruel. Socrates it poisoned, and the Messiah it slew.

We may differ in our opinions as to the cause and origin of this state. You may have your views, I may have mine; but we shall not differ as to the result. Each mind, advancing along its own path of reason and observation, comes to and halts at the same spot. The world is hard: in respect to that we agree. Its very religions have inoculated it with an evil virus, — made it dogmatic, unmerciful, and fierce. In India, a woman's hope of heaven lies over the funeral-pyre of her husband, and from slavery here she passes through smoke and flame to servitude hereafter. Maternal affection — that holiest instinct of the human breast — is converted into an engine of destruction, and the arms which should protect fling the babe into the waters of the

Ganges. Every faith has had its martyrs, every creed been written in blood, and every benediction emphasized by an anathema. The honest convictions of the human heart have in every age been derided, and men have lifted up their voices and shouted in brutal violence over the ashes of human constancy. The best men, as the world counted goodness in the time of Christ, hated Christ the most. The teachers and exponents of God persecuted God the most bitterly when He was manifested in the flesh. He came unto His own, and His own received Him not.

There is nothing sadder than this retrospect of human perversions of divine knowledge and faculties imparted to man. The verdict of man's own acts is against him; and Calvary remains to-day, and ever will remain, the superlative expression of the natural cruelty of man on the one hand, and the tender love of God on the other.

It has been granted us to live in a Christian age and land. The fagot and the torch are behind us. The arena no longer smokes with innocent blood, and the dungeon is no longer regarded as an agent of salvation. And yet, the judgment of the world through other media of expression not unfrequently reveals the same harsh and unmerciful spirit. The Pharisees still live; and were there a Christ there might yet be a cross, and stoning an expression of their creed.

I am to speak to-night of the tenderness and patience of God toward human weakness and human sin. Would that my words might open to your understandings clearer and truer views of the Divine nature than some of you perchance have yet obtained. Would that I might aid you to conceive of your Heavenly Father as He is, — full of forbearance and tender mercies; yearning over you with a love you cannot conceive; drawing nigh to your hearts through His providence and the Gospels, as the sun, through every beam and ray, draws nigh to the earth in spring with gentle ministries of encouragement to growth, and sweet solicitations to fragrance and beauty. Then should you indeed be taught and comforted; then would your natures be quickened and stirred, and all their deep-rooted and wide-branching faculties of thought and feeling thrill with new and vernal expressions of life. The gratitude of our hearts would rise as incense before His throne, and each would say, "The doors of this place have been to me to-night like the gates of heaven and the portals of peace."

It is pleasant for me to minister to you this evening. It is pleasant for me to think that here we can worship and investigate together. Various in the experiences of our lives, various in our intellectual conceptions of God, manifold in our wants, strangers by face; still our thoughts, like waters colored and enriched by the several soils through which they come down to a common junction, can mingle and join in this hour and place. Hail to the hour when differences fade away; when strangers meet as friends; when the long-lost brotherhood of soul with soul, the almost forgotten fellowship in song, the bond of common impulse, is found at last in Christ!

I would first speak of the tenderness of God as shown at certain periods and seasons of our lives.

There are two ways of looking at man morally: one is to regard him as always struggling and always winning; the other, as never struggling and never winning at all. Both of these ways are wrong. On the one hand, there are times of great moral despondency and dejection, — when the soul lies limp and inoperant, when the moral faculties seem benumbed and drugged into fatal lethargy, when the call of duty awakens no response or elicits only rebellion; but there is never a time of stagnation. The soul, like the ocean, is full of currents, and they channel and pierce it with agitations. Life is full of impulses. It is breezy and tremulous; and as the winds of heaven sweep down upon the ocean and ruffle and convulse it, so upon us influences are poured, at the coming and pressure of which we cannot remain passive.

I think that in the heart of almost every man and woman, underneath the covering of forms, underneath the crust of heartless custom, underneath the habit of selfishness, you will find a generous impulse, a desire to grow better and to aid others in worthiness. God has not withdrawn His spirit from mankind. Above us is a moral firmament, and in it that spirit, like a more resplendent sun, is suspended. The rays of its light and warmth penetrate everywhere. They reach and minister to the lowest and coarsest forms of spiritual life. There is not a thought so dark, there is not a wish so ignoble, there is not an ambition so vain, that it is not less dark and ignoble and vain because of this influence. The God of the rose is the God of the bramble as well; and even the thorn-tree must leaf, and sweetness is extorted from the brier. This desire, this generous impulse, must find expression. The warmth above stirs the deadness beneath, and makes barrenness uneasy. And yet, in spite of all this, spiritual dejection comes, despondency and heaviness of heart ensue. We have struggled so much, and won so little; we have fought against circumstances, and by circumstances been defeated; the summit seems so far off, and the path so steep, that our courage fails at times, and we sink in despair. Between the triumph and ourselves are the Garden and the Cross; and, standing alone in the darkness of the night, we wring our hands and cry, "If it be possible, let this cup pass from me!" Sometimes a great temptation circles us on all sides; its circumference of blackness girdles us, and we seek in vain for an outlet to escape. We drop upon our knees in prayer, but prayer brings no relief. We dash madly at the awful belt, but find it to be like a cable of triple steel. We rush frantically from side to side; circumstances conspire in evil conjunction. We are dazed, we are hopeless. The madness of despair seizes upon us, and sinking down we say, "Why struggle longer, — it is in vain? Fate is against me, Heaven is not for me: I can do no more, I can only die."

My friend, don't you die; and never, never cease to contend. When you have reached that position, know that you have come very near God. Weakness is ever near God. He draws nigh to it as a mother draws nigh to a suffering child. What man or woman here, if, when walking at night, you should hear the cry of a deserted babe, would not follow the sound, and, running to the little thing, lift it in your arms and carry it to shelter and care? And do you think God is less merciful than you? Do you think that you can teach Him sympathy, or show Him how to be tender? Do you think that He ever heard a deserted soul crying in the night of its trouble, and does not go to it and lift it to His bosom, and carry it to the light and shelter of His love? If a poor bruised reed is sacred in His sight; if the weak and wounded things in the natural kingdom — the trodden grass, the broken bough, the falling birds — are not beneath His notice, who is he that dares to say the poor bruised soul is not for Him to love, that the prostrate spirit and the breaking heart and the stifled hope are beyond the limit of His care and the reach of His helping hand? Why, consider this in the light of history and revelation a moment.

Who are they that whiten heaven with the flowing of their garments? whose hands lift those ever-vibrating harps? whose heads are crowned and wreathed? whose brows are illuminated with that new name given them of God? Are they not those who came out of great tribulation; whose robes are washed and made white in the blood of the Lamb? Who first followed the Saviour along the path of his ascension, and demonstrated in the sight of heaven the efficacy of the atonement as an act already accomplished? Was it not the thief who hung on the cross? Unto whom was given the keys of the kingdom, the badge of honor and high esteem? Was it not unto him who denied his Lord? Who was appointed to break the boundary of Jewish prejudice; to preach the gospel to the Gentiles, and make it free as the water that runs and the light that shines? Was it not Paul, the persecutor of Jesus? And whose heart here to-night is fullest of gratitude? whose lips beyond the grave will open quickest in thanksgiving? — whose? Of that one among us whose darkness was the most dense when the light of mercy broke through and illumined it!

No, no, my friend, don't you despair; there's hope in your future yet. There is not a hand's-breadth of sky between you and the grave to-day that is not of azure so long as in your heart lingers one regret for sin, one desire of doing good, — one longing for God, one hope of moral mastery. Put yourself in the right, then endure unto the end, and you *shall* be saved. What a joy it is to preach a gospel of hope to you!

Again I would remark, that if the bruised reed may represent our broken hopes, it may also represent our broken resolutions.

I have said already that our lives morally were marked with fluctuations. Our feelings rise and sink like waves of the sea. If at one moment we gain the wished-for elevation, the next we are shaken from it as a bird is blown from the topmost branches of an exposed tree when a gust strikes it. And yet how noble is the mind of man in its conceptions! How far it can flash its thoughts! Along what interminable lines, across what vast spaces, the intellect can pursue its investigations! How exalted those emotions which inspire the soul at times, and lift it as on mighty and invisible wings above the earth and earthly surroundings! You have all had these moods, —

these reachings out and elevation of feeling. You have had longings and dissatisfactions with self, and travailed in the birth of strong desires, begotten of God, to be better and accomplish more good. And you have more than once resolved that it should be so. In the street, in the office, and in the chamber, in the closet, in company, or alone with yourselves, conscience has smitten you, and you have said, "This thing must stop. I will change my course to-day, and be no more as I have been." And some of you can date a great change from such moments,—such a change as comes over a rose when it blossoms, or over the heavens when the rising wind sweeps it free from clouds.

I believe every soul has such moments of conviction and resolution,—moments when more by far than we can see depends upon how we act; when our own happiness and the happiness of others hang poised on the decision of a moment. It takes but an instant and a single revolution of the wheel to turn the ship, but by that movement it is decided whether she shall anchor on this side of the globe or on that. It takes but an instant for the mind to act, yet in the passing of a thought it is often settled what will be the direction and issue of a life.

Now the past is full of such experience; such seasons of introspection and resolution have come to us all. Time and again have our souls mounted from the low level of our lives, like a lark tremulous with song; but no sooner had we poured forth the raptures of the passing impulse, than we dropped again into the marsh, and were ashamed at our own fickleness.

Now, friends, God, as I conceive, is never nearer to one than when he stands dissatisfied with himself and manner of life, and longs to be better. When the mind is about to make a needed resolution, God invariably draws nigh to help it. Because you have broken one resolution, never imagine that He will not assist you to keep another, made with greater wisdom and a more determined purpose. The temples of God, so far as we represent them, are all constructed out of ruins. He builds from the fragments of an ancient overthrow. Be persuaded of this, that nothing good in you ever escapes the notice of God. He is not, as some seem to picture him, a heartless overseer, standing over you whip in hand, and watching for a chance to get in a blow. His observation is like a gardener's. There is not a bud of promise that can open in your soul, there is not an odor that can be added to the fragrance of your lives, that he does not detect it and rejoice in it. Whatever beautifies you glorifies Him. He delights in your development, and smiles on your every effort in that direction. God is always ready to give a man one more chance. The world is hard and smiting in its judgments, and swift as lightning in its censure; and its condemnation falls on a man as a huge beam of timber falls on the body, crushing it down to the ground and holding it there; but God is slow to wrath, full of forbearance and tender mercies. He prunes away the dead and soggy branches, He transplants and grafts; but He never cuts a tree of productive nature down, yea, after three years of barrenness the tree has yet one more year of grace, and the last year is fuller of care and nurture and enticements to fruitfulness, than all the others.

Now, I suppose that if the good resolutions we have formed and broken were represented materially to the eye, we should all appear to those that gazed upon us as standing amid fragments of former beauty and the cast-up foundations of former strength; and I suppose that morally we do so appear in the sight of God to-night. And the spectacle of our dejection and overthrow, of our failure and prostration, of our ruin and despair, stirs him with pity, and awakens all his mercy and compassion in our behalf. And if there is one here who is worse off morally than the rest of us, — one who stands more bewildered and hopeless amid the *debris* of the commandments he has broken, — one who is more scarred and bruised than the majority of us, — God by an election of mercy draws nighest to that soul, and through the prayers and hymns and words of this service, the memories and uses of this day, He seeks to encourage that man to renewed spiritual effort and inspire him with hope to try again. Why with hope? Because no man ever attempts anything without hope. There is not the least element of heavenly progress in despair, and the first thing the Spirit of God seeks to stir in the soul is a great expectation of a coming good. That Divine influence comes out of the heavens upon a soul as a strong current of air, after a day of fog and storm, comes out of the west, clears up the clouded horizon of his life, sweeps the long-gathered and thickening darkness from over his head, and brightens the firmament with stars. Would that one and another of you here might feel this Divine Spirit coming to you in this manner to-night, feel the atmosphere of your sluggish or stormy lives vibrate to the incoming of such change-working influences, and that ahead of you were years of sunlit effort, and at the close an hour of radiant decline! In this spirit of hope or prophecy — I know not which — I point you all to lives nobler than you have thus far lived, to a moral elevation of feeling higher than you have thus far experienced, to sympathies for man wider, deeper, more generous than any you have thus far felt, — to a consecration of all your powers to God's service, and to an hour at last of spiritual victory and supreme reward.

And I want you all to feel,—because it is *true,*—that all this is made possible through the tender love of God for you, as revealed by analogy in nature, and more fully yet, as through a more perfect medium, in the life and death of his only-begotten Son, Christ Jesus our Lord.

This passage, this quotation from the Old Testament in order to illustrate the spirit of the New, suggests to my mind another thought, which grows, as I live, more and more delightful to me. It is this: that Christ does not and will not apply the least force or violence to propagate his law or religion.

Now, if there is one thing that my mind revolts at more than another, it is at any rude and violent interference with its independence, with the law and order of its free action. If religion meant surrender of intellectual freedom, if it meant subjugation of any faculty to superior power, if it meant bondage of thought and terror of motive, there is not a principle in my nature which would not rise up in arms against it. Heaven must not be made to appear to my mind as a vast corral, into which souls like cattle are stampeded by force or fear. And I know not of any style of speech more obnoxious to me than that which presents nothing higher, nothing nobler to men, to inspire them with religious tendencies than the motive of fear. The horror of hell can furnish no well-regulated mind with an impulse toward heaven. And a preacher who appeals to fear, to sheer cowardice, in his audience, is unfit to proclaim the Gospel of Christ. Such a speaker perverts and belittles the Gospels. He insults intelligence. He can find no warrant for his monstrous misinterpretation of God, and outrage on intellectual laws, in the teachings and conduct of Christ or the Apostles. Why, you might as well try to frighten a flower into lifting its face toward the sun as to frighten a soul into lifting itself toward God! The attraction of light and love from above, and not the propulsion of fear from beneath, is what accomplishes the beautiful result. There is no need of any such rude and tyrannous force, such violent benevolence. In the soul are certain capacities and affinities, and God is to them their natural object of love and service. To clear away the obstructions which Satan has pushed up between the soul and God, to enlighten the understanding and thereby correct the judgment, to interpret God properly to the mind and heart of the hearer, is the preacher's duty and the preacher's joy. To send each hearer away at the close of a service feeling that he is thankful that the heavens are what they are, and God is what he is, and he himself is as he is, save as to his sin, is the highest triumph of preaching. Why, you cannot frighten man even in the inclination of his appetites. You cannot break down and disrupt by force even the bulwark of his sensations. If any particular species of fruit — a pear, for instance — is distasteful to a person, you cannot annul by force or fear the law of his sensations; you can, indeed, compel him to eat it, but it is repugnant nevertheless, and yields no satisfaction to his taste; and if man, along the lower ranges of his nature, thus defies your insane attempt at compulsion, do you imagine that you can conquer him by the same method along the higher? If you cannot subjugate his body, the weak and perishable part of him, do you conceive that you can subdue his mind and soul, and the mighty and immortal faculties of his being?

Now God, inasmuch as he is our Creator, understands the structure and law of our minds, and never offers the least violence to their free exercise. Indeed, our independence is his glory; and the unforced, spontaneous character of our obedience and praise is what gives them the chief value in his sight. No, my friend, God will use no compulsion with you. He loads neither scale of the balance. You sit your throne of self-sovereignty in undisturbed possession. You are free in the exercise of your volition, — free as God himself. Your salvation or damnation will be the result of your own voluntary act. To-night your feet are at the fork of two roads: the one is narrow and straight, and few there be that tread it, but those who walk it are walking forever upward; the other is wide and crooked, and multitudes throng it, but those who wheel and rush along that populous road are going downward. Some of you, I say, stand at the fork of these divergent roads this evening; and you are free, perfectly free, to enter either. Pause and reflect before you take your next step, for that may decide the entire journey. I wonder which path you are deciding to enter!

Have you ever thought how many weak things there are in the world? Look at the natural kingdom. How few are the oaks and how many are the rushes! There is a rose, with a stem so fragile as to almost break under the burden of its own blushing and fragrant bloom. Yet God is God of the reed and the rose. There is not a spire of grass bruised by the trampling foot; there is not a leaf fluttering from a twig; there is not a bird that flies nor a worm that crawls, — no, nor any order of created life, — so low and weak as to be beneath His care. Now look at man. Look at society in its component parts. Consider men and women as they live and move to-day. Are they strong or weak? are they happy or sad? are they joyful or do they need comfort? Why, friends, I sometimes think that there is no such thing as happiness in the world. So much disappointment, so much misery, so much concealed pain, so many hidden sorrows, so much studiously covered wretchedness, comes to my knowledge that I almost lose hope and heart at times, and feel like crying out: "Society is a vast charnel-house, where everything that is bright in hope or cheerful in expectation lies buried. Life is a monstrous disappointment, and death the only portal to peace." There is not a day that passes in which virtue does not sell itself for bread; in which some poor, harassed, or frenzied creature does not rush madly upon death; in which the good are not persecuted and the weak trampled upon. Behind windows you look at heedlessly, tragedies red as history or fiction ever painted are being acted, and faces you admire mask with smiles an inward torture worse than the agony of the rack. Who, even in this audience, has realized the fulfilment of his early hope? Whose life has not its mortifications, its bitter concealments, its studied evasions, its poignant humiliations, its wild uneasiness, its wrestlings and defeat? But we do not represent life; we represent only the fairest portions and the highest level of it. Below us are the great masses of humanity, and they writhe and moan and weep, they toil and starve and curse and fight and die. The world goes roaring on as heedless of those who fall as the gale in autumn is heedless of the leaves it strips from the tree, or the branches it wrenches away. But God is mindful of it all; he notes it all, and I would fain think that, in the infinite resources of healing, is balm for all. "Come unto me, all ye who labor and are heavy laden, and I will give you rest." What a promise that is! He will not sell it to us, nor loan it to us: he *gives* it to us. And what a reach and stretch there is in the assurance, "Come unto me *all* ye"! It includes every one. Not the rich, not the refined, not the pure, but the poor and the coarse, the fallen and the weak; those who have been wrecked by others, and those who have wrecked themselves,—*all* can have *rest*. Rest! Who gets rest in this life, outside of God? Whose mind gets rest? Whose soul gets it? Does the ocean get rest? Does the wind get it? Does the torrent find repose? Yes. For the ocean has its calms, and the wind lulls, and the torrent in summer ceases to roar; but the life of man is rougher than the sea, and fiercer than the wind, and more headlong than the torrent, and in himself man finds no rest, and no repose, and no season for repose, until the vault darkens over his head and that long night with its dreamless sleep comes on. And God sees all this and feels it all, and the beat of his sympathy is without intermission.

Now there are a great many things that tend to keep us from God, but nothing, no, nor all other hindrances put together, so much as wrong views of God. There is a girl whose virtue lies like a soiled and trampled flower, unable to lift itself. She cannot go to God, because her purity is gone.

"God is white," she says, "and how can I go to whiteness?" There is a man of business, who will not be a Christian because he has no time. As if it took time to inhale the perfume of a bank of violets, when the wind blows it into your very face. Here is another down upon whose faith and hope and life a great blast of tribulation has swooped, and torn everything up by the roots, and prostrated all the growth of twenty years of religious education; and, standing over the grave or in the empty house, she wrings her hands, and cries out: "There is no God in the heavens, or if there is, he is hard and harsh and cruel, for he has taken from me my husband and all my children at one rude blow!" I met a man the other day who had lived like the prodigal; wasted the substance of body and brain in riotous living. A magnificent wreck he was. A man who stood as I have seen a tree stand after a fire had swept through the forest, — blasted and charred to the very core, all the life and vigor burnt out of it; yet keeping its magnificent girth and symmetry of proportion, even to the topmost bough. So that man stood. I took him kindly by the hand, and said, "Friend, there is hope in your future yet." He drew himself slowly up until he stood at his straightest, looked me steadily in the eye, and said, "Do you mean to say, Mr. Murray, that if I went to-night to God, He would pardon such a wretch as I?"

See how he misunderstood God! See how we all misunderstand Him! Pardon! Is there any one He will not pardon? Is there a noisome marsh or stagnant pool on the face of the whole earth so dark, so reeking with rottenness and mire, that the sun scorns to shine on it? and is there a man so low, so heavy with corruption, so coarse and brutal that God's love does not seek him out? How is the world to be redeemed if you put a limit to God's love? How is the great mass of humanity to be washed and lifted if the thoughts of God are like our thoughts, and His ways like our ways? It is because He does not love as we do, because He does not feel as we do, because He does not act as we do, that I have any hope for my race, — that I have any hope for myself.

A bruised reed He will not break. Let our thoughts, like a song, close with the sweetness of the opening note. As those who, leaving home in winter when all is bleak and drear, come back in spring to find the trees in blossom, and the earth exhaling odors, and everything more lovely than when they left; so I would call your minds back to the assurance of the Scriptures, the tenderness of God, and the opening thought of our discourse. This evening we have been permitted to meet in this place for worship. Let it stand in your remembrance as the expression of His love. This is the sabbath hour; let it be remembered as the hour in which so many of us worshipped and adored together. Are we strangers? No, we are friends, and the day and audience warrant the word. The bitterness, the jealousies, the rivalries, the piques, the misconceptions to which life has exposed us, die out in our hearts as we sit here together; a tenderness not unlike the tenderness of God steals into our bosoms. The throb of mutual sympathy, the lifting of common prayer, the aspiration for a higher life, bind us together. Who wishes ill to any? None. Who remembereth ill done or ill received, save to forgive or ask to be forgiven? Not one. We yield our hands to the clasp of a universal brotherhood, and our thoughts fly out in love toward the poor and the ignorant, the weak, the sinful, and the lowly, the world over. God pity them all; and most of all we pray that He may use us to make His tenderness and mercy known to them.

And thus I commend you all to the tenderness of God. May the thought of it comfort you when you need comfort, and strengthen you when you need strength! And when you shall meet at last face to face what men most dread, but which I do not doubt shall prove to many of you here your best friend, may the same tenderness be over you as the face of a mother is over her waking child. This earth is not our home. God is beckoning us onward. We shall depart. We shall pass into forgetfulness. We shall sleep. We shall be changed. Into what we know not; but this we know, that we shall be satisfied when we awake in his likeness. What will that waking, what will that likeness, be?

SERMON II.

THE UNION OF MORAL FORCES.

"Glory to God in the highest, and on earth peace, good-will toward men." — LUKE ii. 14.

AS a matter of history this verse is exceedingly interesting. It shows us how the birth of our Redeemer was celebrated. Heaven recognized the magnitude of the event, and through its representatives congratulated the earth. Toward God the attitude of heaven was that of praise, — praise of His love and wisdom and power. Toward the earth it was one of sympathy and felicitation. The angels appreciated the value of that birth to man, and predicted the era of universal peace and good-will. In this the angels only expressed what the Scriptures everywhere confirm; what Christ loved to say of Himself, what the prophets said of Him from the beginning; what the Apostles wrote, and John foresaw. If ever peace was made visible in outward form, it was in the person of our blessed Lord; if ever good-will to man found expression, it did in the life and teachings of Christ; and whether you look at the influence of His deeds or His nature, we can in very truth assert that "of His peace there is no end."

Previous to Christ there was no peace, either in principle or expression, among men. War was the normal condition and practice of mankind. The strong ruled the weak. The world was divided into two classes, — oppressors and slaves. Wrong had become systematized. Civil government, which should be a fountain of peace, was a source of war; and nations were as wild animals that have no law but their appetites and their fears.

Men in their individual relations were antagonistic and rude. Humane impulse had not been born. Brotherly love, as of one stock and race, was unknown. The Jew hated the Gentile, and the Gentile retaliated on the Jew. Even religion begat animosities, and men inspired by it became cruel and perverse.

Now, Christ came to change all this, and the angelic heralds truly proclaimed his mission. He came to introduce a new and higher order of life and feeling, — to awaken the dormant power of sympathy in man, — to bridge the chasm of hatred which divided nations and races, and bring them at last to the acknowledgment and practice of universal brotherhood.

I propose to discuss before you to-night the subject of Peace and Good-Will among men, and the result to which they would lead. I must omit the national relations of it, although they are worthy of attention. God works up through the individual to the nation, and through one nation to all nations. This is the law, the drift and tendency of His administration, and I have no doubt but that eventually all differences between nations will be settled by friendly arbitration, and not as now by the sword. But I must pass this point by this evening. I wish to notice, in the first place, the personal and church relations of the subject, and remark upon the cheering progress which is being made toward union of all moral forces in society, and the harmonizing of all differences which provoke discord and enmity. Secondly, I shall allude to the relation of this principle to us as individual Christians, and show how and when we shall find peace.

Now, any one who observes the present state of things about us must see that the good are not united as the bad are. Evil has a coherence, a unity, a oneness of purpose and combination of energies, to which goodness has not as yet attained. The wicked all pull one way, and they pull with all their might. Wickedness is always unanimous, and self-collected, and at peace with itself. The Devil never rejects any help, come from what source it may. He welcomes direct, and he welcomes indirect assistance also. Whatever can debauch men, whatever can lead them astray, whoever will assist him by little or by much, is accepted and enrolled among his forces. By this process, by thus utilizing every agent and agency, he is enabled to accomplish vast results, and keep his seat and throne in the world. It is not so with the good. They have not as yet learned the lesson of combination, the power which lies in organization and unity of effort. If a man or organization is half wrong, Satan utilizes that half, and works it in somehow to advance his schemes of mischief; but if a man or organization is only half good, good men stand off and look askant at it and say: "No, we cannot affiliate with that; we must not have anything to do with it lest we are misunderstood, lest we hazard our influence." And so the sum total of correct influence in society is lessened.

The good are thus divided and separated one from another; differences are perpetuated, and union and peace deferred. You may take this city for an illustration, — and it supplies us with a good one too. Here lines are drawn; and one class of power stands on this side, and another on that. One man says, "This view of God is the true view," and will have nothing to do with another who disputes it. And so it comes about that we are fighting evil here in companies and squads, and under a dozen leaders, and not by regiments and brigades and divisions, all under one leader, assisted by co-operation of all his forces. Not only so, but some good people seem afraid lest old differences should not continue, and the old suicidal and wicked division of moral forces endure. They seem to think that to be faithful to truth they must keep knocking somebody down, or be continually knocked down themselves, and that, if opposition to them should cease, and former opponents begin to coalesce with them, the truth for which they have so long struggled would in some way be endangered, and their relation to it changed.

Why, I am astonished at the way some men talk and act. There is a certain class of orthodox Christians in this city, who seem to be afraid to have any one outside of their own sect agree with them. They have made orthodoxy consist so much in theological opposition that they are frightened to see those who have held different views begin to harmonize with them. If a man preaches the Gospel with such demonstration of love and spiritual power that it reaches the heart, and a person supposed to be a Unitarian says, "That's good preaching enough for me," they begin at once to be suspicious of the preaching and the preacher. Just as if bitterness and difference and wrangling were to continue forever in this city! just as if God had nothing in store for us here but perpetual alienation, division, and hostility! I do not believe any such monstrous prediction as that. The world moves; and it moves, as impelled by God's spirit, toward harmony and peace, and a union of moral forces, here and the world over, under one banner, in order to accomplish certain blessed and needed results. For one, I hail, as an auspicious omen, these symptoms of returning good sense and correct views and loving fellowship together under Christ. I would go farther to find one point of agreement with a good man than to discover five of difference. My brother, in love to man and faith toward God,—brother still, although differing in views,—tell me what you hold in common with me; tell me where and how we can join hands to teach the ignorant, and clothe the naked, and feed the starving, and reform the vicious; and leave whatever difference there may be between us for God to settle and explain when we have entered His presence. There is such a thing as a man standing so straight as to fall over backward, and it is possible for a Christian to make so much of his denomination or his creed as to forget the Gospels. The Puritans were orthodox enough, but they were not precisely such models as we should follow in their treatment of dissentients. They drew their inspiration from the Jewish rather than the Christian dispensation. The Old Testament and not the New, misapplied and perverted, was the baleful torch with which they lighted their witch-fires.

Now it seems to me perfectly natural that men

who have opposed evangelical religion should gradually drop their opposition and begin to harmonize with it. A vast deal of opposition to orthodox opinion in this city springs from a gross ignorance of what it teaches and its holders believe. Men have been educated to believe a slander and a lie. They have been educated to believe that we of evangelical views preach "that hell is paved with infants' skulls," — that "men by nature are as bad as devils, as bad as they can be," — and other enormous and outrageous propositions, which no orthodox preacher preaches or believes. And when, one by one, they are undeceived; when they hear us preach of the love and tenderness of God for human kind; when they hear us preach a gospel of hope, of love for others, of cheerfulness and progression, they are surprised and say, "Well now, if that is orthodox preaching, then I am orthodox."

There is another thought in this connection, and I am glad to call your attention to it, for it requires frankness on my part to suggest, and candor on your part to consider it. The great joy of my public life is that I am in a city where free speech in America was born, where it has been nurtured, and where it still thrives. Your intelligence is such that you not only do not fear, but you desire the freest utterance on the part of your speakers, the fullest discussion of passing events; your city has been the theatre of a great religious revolution; some of you can remember perhaps the earthquake which shook the doctrinal structure of many churches to the ground. You heard the crash and the shouting which followed. And now another great movement is beginning to make itself felt. Men who have been trying to build a house without mortar and without brick are beginning to search for the old foundations, if peradventure they may find, in modified form, some basis for their faith to stand on. I doubt whether men were ever more dissatisfied with the old faith than they are with the new, ever more adrift and uneasy within themselves as to what to believe. Seventy years of experiment have demonstrated that negation is not religion, that scepticism is no adequate equivalent for faith, and that men who can do nothing but tear away and pull down and destroy are no fit guides to those who believe in right and wrong and the immortality of the soul. And we who attempt to discuss these matters, whom you have chosen as your watchmen, are bound to tell you how the heavens look and which way the wind blows.

Well, the thought which I would suggest is this: It is the law that all revolts from established order of thought should go first to extremes, and then to gradually correct themselves. Men do not at once see the logical results of revolution. They do not see that anarchy is removed but a single step from independence. When this city broke away from the position of the fathers, many of the prime movers in that theological stampede never dreamed to what madness their followers would go. Channing never dreamed of a Frothingham. I speak from the evangelical stand-point, of course, and I say, that there are thousands of Unitarians, so called, in this city to-day, — men and women of holy lives, who love the Bible as much as we do, — who are appalled at the radical wing of their denomination. They see as plainly as we — no one with eyes can help seeing it — that the drift and tendency of their teaching is toward infidelity and the baldest scepticism. They are alarmed, and, like merchantmen that have discovered a pirate in the fleet, begin to draw off. They are not prepared to throw overboard the Scriptures, to call Christ nothing more than John Jones, to dig a pit and cast their long-cherished hopes of heaven into it; and their natural inclination, the logical tendency of their position, is to get back to safer ground. I verily believe that a practical, if not a nominal, union will erelong be made between this class of Unitarians and the great body of evangelical believers. The date of that happy event may be retarded by unforeseen circumstances, by pride and perversity on either side; but it is bound to come. Over our graves our children will join their hands and the Commonwealth, to found which the fathers labored and died, will stand, the disastrous schism healed, clothed once more in the unity of her ancestral and triumphant faith.

Come, then, Peace, and breathe upon us! Come, as the wind comes from the south, warm as the touch and fragrant as the breath of love! Come, as the dove came to the ark, bearing with thee the symbol and evidence that the waters of death are ebbing, and a new world of promise is rising into sight! Come, as the angels came at the birth of Christ, and tell us once more of peace and good-will to men!

There are other reasons than those I have mentioned for this hope, among which is this, — that similarity of labors begets similarity of feeling, and results in a practical union. Men are looking and planning for the union of all denominations, on the ground of doctrinal unanimity. They think that this denomination will give up one point, and another some other; that each in the interest of union will pare off some denominational corner, and shade down to a common hue some exceptional color, until at last everybody will think alike. My friends, that day will never come; at least, it is too remote for us of this generation to debate. It is a dream, to the fulfilment of which the structure of the human mind itself is opposed. Men will never think on any one topic precisely alike. They cannot look at truth from exactly the same point of view, any more than a hundred persons can look at an oil painting from precisely the same angle of vision. The light and shade will not appear the same to each. Education, temperament, predilections, amounting often almost to a prejudice,—these will come in and cause divergence of opinion. So long as the Bible is a necessity, so long will different interpretations be patronized. While we see God through a glass darkly, our views of Him will vary, because dimness and the moving of many shadows are between us and Him. Not until we have risen above the heavy atmospheres of this mortal life,—not until, through the crystalline medium of heaven, we behold Him face to face, and from that altitude, with holy and instructed vision, see all the outgoings of His nature, all the sequence of His doings, from beginning to end, shall we see Him as with one eye. In the light of that demonstration differences will fade away, and the multitude of the redeemed will stand, hand clasped in hand, around a common throne. But until that day, my friends, I look for no intellectual unity. While theology is a science, and knowledge of God depends on human, and hence fallible and conflicting, interpretations, men will continue to differ in religious matters. Doctrinally they will stand apart from and opposed to each other. When we see God face to face, we shall all see Him alike, and not until then.

No. The path of union and peace in the religious world lies not in that direction. Individual opinions will obtrude their obstructions in front of us in the future as in the past. They cannot be levelled and graded down. You cannot make a composite of men's conflicting views, and macadamize the future so that the world will roll onward and upward without a jolt or jar. The true and only practical ground of union is found in union of effort, and not union of views ; in oneness of feeling, and not oneness of opinions; in similarity of conduct, and not similarity of belief. The Methodist, so far as his head goes, will be a Methodist still, the Baptist a Baptist, and the Unitarian a Unitarian; but in heart, in purpose, in hope of heaven, in labors for man, in the emotional and benevolent energies of our natures, we find our union. Recruited from many States, — of complex opinions, — differing in our views as to the causes of the rebellion, and how the campaign should be fought out,—agreeing only in this, that we are willing to unite and act together as against a common enemy, we put ourselves under one Leader, blind to all else save this, that the banner over us is love. This is a union to be desired; this is such a union as it is our duty to have; and this, thank God, is nearly ours.

Men say that I am hopeful, and so I am ; but

my hope is not a vain dream, a poetical aspiration. It is a hope born of knowledge; it is based upon the apprehension of a law, — a law which I trace through all the pages of history as a man traces a golden thread through a piece of cloth which is being unrolled before his eyes. The law is this: That the world has moved onward and upward by an accelerated motion and ever-multiplying accumulation of forces. The driving power has increased as the train has gone thundering on; and never did good influences move so fast, never did they control and shape so many, as they do to-day. The progress made toward union and peace in religious matters, in the last two centuries, is a matter of astonishment. A few facts will illustrate this to your satisfaction, and show you with what long and rapid strides we have advanced.

Two hundred years ago tyranny ruled here, and the worst kind of tyranny at that; for it was tyranny, not over men's bodies, but over their minds. About all the religious freedom the Puritans knew was, "Think as we do, or suffer the consequences."

Two hundred years ago two men were tied to the tail of a cart, and whipped through your streets with knotted lashes, — "with all the power the hangman could put forth," as the record says, — their mouths being stopped with wooden gags to prevent their cries of agony from being heard. And what, pray, was their offence? Simply and solely because they were Quakers! A woman, — and a recent mother at that, — with her babe in her arms, was tied to the whipping-post which stood on the Common, near the corner of West Street, and beaten nearly to death. And why? Because she was a Quakeress. And when released from that brutal violence, she dropped upon her knees, poor woman, and prayed that God would forgive her persecutors, and bring, at last, a day of liberty and peace to this city.

That day is come. It is here, and we are living in it; and the soul of that saintly Quakeress looks down from heaven, and sees the fulfilment of her prayers this evening, and rejoices at the sight!

Two hundred years ago, within a stone's-throw of Tremont Temple, where Brother Fulton is preaching, a man was cruelly and publicly whipped for being a Baptist.

Why do I mention these things? Simply that you may realize the progress which the world has made in the last two centuries toward union and peace; that you may see that, when one expresses the belief that not many years hence all who obey God and love their fellow-men shall stand together, he does not deal in extravagant speech, but makes a prediction which all history warrants and renders probable. I tell you, friends, the old warfares, one by one, are dying out. The sounds of bitter contention are being hushed. Death is gradually bringing a conclusion to past bitterness, and traces of conflict are being covered by the grass which grows on graves. We are all moving, as a ship, after a period of storm, goes moving into the west. The clouds are broken and rolled upward. The sea and sky are crimson, every sail is a sheet of orange, every rope a line of gold. And so it moves along its path of emerald, crested with fire, gathering a deeper glory as it moves, until the winds die out, the waters sleep, and night, brilliant with stars, settles over the tranquil sea.

Not only does the course of history corroborate this view, but the very nature of the case makes it probable. Why, what is the great aim of the Gospel? What is its drift and tendency? To separate and antagonize the good? to divorce and divide and set one in array against another? No; the tendency of Christianity is to bring the good together. Christ is as a great magnet, and those who feel the attraction of His name and spirit converge and are drawn nearer together themselves, being drawn nearer to Him. When we sing "Nearer, my God, to Thee," we petition not only nearness to Him, but also nearness to all His creatures. The good of all ages and climes belong, in a peculiar sense, to each other. Not one of all that vast multitude who died at the stake; not one of the thousands who laid down their lives for liberty; not one of that long list who died before the dawn of the day in which we now rejoice, sighing for light; not a man or woman is striving or dying for man's good to-day, but that is knit and united to me. I appropriate the spirit as truly as the results of their lives. For what is history, — for what civilization, — for what the arts and appliances of letters, — for what the element of sympathy in man, — if not to unite us to the great and the good of all time? I anticipate the fellowship of the pure that shall be mine in heaven, as the gardener anticipates the rich perfume of the blossom by the first suggestion of fragrance in the bud. We enroll ourselves in the great fraternity of God's children on earth before we enter the fellowship of His children in heaven.

My friends, as the power of the Spirit is more and more felt in our hearts, so will this Divine unity of love between all the good be more realized in our souls. It is not for me to say who will feel it, it is not for me to say who is worthy; but all who are worthy will feel it. Names will continue to exist, nominal distinctions will survive; but, deeper than all, dearer than all, the unity of the Spirit will be felt. We shall still abide each in his own house, but the intercourse of love and community of feeling will exist untrammelled and unchecked. From the ashes of former differences peace shall spring, more perfect in plumage, sweeter in song, than the Phœnix of the classics, and man shall be to his fellow-man a brother.

Now, having spoken of the union and peace which are to be experienced among masses of men, — of that "bond of perfectness" which is to unite and adorn the pure and good, supplanting present alienation and difference, I would allude to the second point, and direct the application of my theme and text to individuals.

I remark, then, that Christianity produces a union of the powers and energies of the individual soul.

The soul, — by which I mean all the operant faculties of man's nature, — is now divided, and half is hostile to half.

Take any man or woman in this audience;— let any one of you analyze your emotions, recall your past; and you will find that, since the birth of conscience in you, you have been at war with yourself, your soul has been the arena of conflict. Duty and inclination have been at war. Your very emotions have joined in the unnatural contest, and often risen in rebellion against what you knew was right. The good in you has held its own, as a man holds his own in battle, fighting against odds, at the point of the bayonet. My hearers, I do not say that there are none who float through life, — men and women who do not struggle, have few temptations, make few falls: some may be protected by circumstance; some, by their very weakness and lack of fibre, may have stood unhurt, as grasses stand, when the gale overhead is wringing and wrenching the branches from the oaks, and riving them to the very heart. But natures that have any girth to them, any upward reach, any latitude of emotion, any tree-like formation, are exposed to pressure, — are often made the sport of converging currents and riotous forces. Such natures are constantly agitated and blown about, and full of writhing and groaning. In this category most of the race, and I presume most of you to whom I am speaking, belong. You have not floated through life as a feather floats upon the evening air; nor will you sink, as that feather falls, unknown and unnoted, into forgetfulness. In different spheres of labor and life you have toiled and suffered; you have made your wealth or daily support, not by luck, but by years of application; you have done some good, and wrought some evil, and the war between the higher and lower parts of your nature still wages. Even this blessed Sabbath is not so much a day of rest as a breathing-spell; for to-morrow, and all the days ahead, will be full of panting and struggle, until breath fails and the conflict is over forever.

Now I want to speak to you who have been tossed and buffeted amid the conflicting experiences of life; and I want you to feel that every word comes directly from my heart to your hearts, that my soul speaks to your souls; and I say to you, my brother and sister, that all you have felt and suffered, and borne up against, and been prostrated by, was a part of God's merciful dealings with you. He has blown and buffeted you, he has wrung and wrenched you, that he might teach you the lesson of your weakness and dependence. You have been honored by chastisement; you have been strengthened by opposition; you have been glorified through suffering. When you draw nigh to heaven, you will draw nigh to it, it is true, as ships creep into harbors after a night of storm,—their masts broken, their sails in tatters, and their decks all littered with wreck; but you will enter it with hymns of praise and thanksgiving for your deliverance. Nor will you lack welcome. Heaven is full of sympathy for such as barely escape wreck; and the shining shore will shine all the brighter because of the glorified faces that shall throng it as your souls are floated up toward the golden marge.

And you must also feel that, even in this life, victory, in part, will be yours. As the days pass, you will find that, as a reward for virtuous effort, self-mastery is slowly but surely coming to you.

Every tempest will cause you to root yourself deeper in, and twine yourself more closely around, Christ as the great, immovable Rock of your salvation. And when that last and strongest gale — which blows for all, and overturns many — shall bear down upon you, the unification of all your powers having been completed, and with every thought and purpose and hope of your heart purged and perfected, you will stand triumphant, exclaiming, "O death, where is thy sting? O grave, where is thy victory?"

But, my friend, where will you be in that hour, — you who have no Saviour to whom to cling, — where? — No, I will not tell you. What does your heart say? What does your conscience say? What does the Bible say?

You see, my hearers, what gateway leads to peace. The hope, the only hope of it, is Christ, the author of all peace, in you, working out the peaceable fruits of righteousness. Through faith in Him, and in the direction of God's providential dealings, the good in your natures gains the ascendant, and the evil gradually retires. Stone by stone, and block by block, the temple of your hope is rising. Every stone represents a struggle, every block a mighty effort. Without God you would never have started to build, and without Him you can never even now finish. If any soul here is looking for peace in any other direction, if he thinks it will come to him in any other way, that soul will surely be mistaken. You must fight and pray if you would win. The cross, by the law of God's appointment, precedes the crown. These are trite sayings; but they express a truth which underlies all Christian hope and inspires all Christian effort.

But, friends, do all you may, fight bravely as you may, still victory will come only at the setting of the sun. The land of peace lies on the other side of the grave. That is the outer door of sombre surface, behind which the gates of solid pearl emit their splendor. Never let your minds dwell on the grave, — that gateway to a happier world, — as over something dark and repellant. In ignorance the world draped it in sable, and made their funeral gatherings around it with lamentations. Nothing short of the resurrection of Christ could have dispelled this fear, and stemmed the tide of human superstition. In His death He made a greater revelation than in His life.

The tomb had been from the beginning the terror of the world, — a deep, dark, impenetrable mystery. But Christ did not shrink. He went down into the shadow of its silence; explored its unknown recesses; felt His way along the crumbling edge of His mortality; threaded the labyrinth to its farthest extremity; and, reascending to the light, the world beheld Him again. But how did they behold Him? They beheld Him leading captivity captive!

He was sown in weakness, but He was raised in power: He was sown in dishonor, but He was raised in glory.

In the light of that investigation and that result we know what the grave is, and its relation to the good.

The world is full of failures which this life can never retrieve. Many of you have lost what you will never find on the earth, for the waves of death have cast it high up on the farther shore. Some of you have missed what you most purely longed for; the songs you might have sung fail in your throat, and laughter serves to prevent a groan. Your early hopes have not been realized, and you are now too old to hope. The strings of the harp are broken, and it is now too late in the night to retune the tangled cords.

But, friends, let no one of you, in such straits, be overmuch discouraged or cast down. Peace will yet come to you. Death will bring to you the opportunity of a new start. The conditions of this mortal life will not pursue you beyond the grave. All that hindered, all that burdened, all that vexed you here, will be no longer felt. In the quiet of its shadow, in the fulness of life beyond, the wicked cease from troubling and the weary are at rest.

Thus, by the gradual rectification of our natures and the unification of all our powers in holiness, and then — as the finishing and perfecting providence — the change which death shall work in our condition, mankind at last will find their peace. Thus God's great plan in Christ, of which the Angels sang, shall be consummated, and peace shall be on earth and good-will to man.

But what is the cause of this peace, and through what medium does it primarily come to us? I answer, that the love of God is the cause, and belief in Christ is the medium through which it comes to every heart that opens to receive it.

There is not a man, there is not a woman, there is not a youth, in this audience this evening, I care not how widely you have wandered, nor how deeply you have sinned, nor how great has been your rebellion, to whom God in his love does not come and offer this peace, as secured to you in the death of your Saviour. Only drop your hostility, only forego your rebellion, only throw down your arms, only utter a cry, only make a sign, he says, and I will pardon you here and now. This is the love of God to you, my hearers, as held by the Evangelical churches. Was there ever a love like unto it? Think of your life, now far spent perhaps, — your life of neglect, of indifference, of ingratitude, of opposition, and then tell me if you have ever known, in father or mother, in husband or wife, in any friend living or dead, a love to be compared to this Divine love for you? There are faces back of me over which as they sleep the evergreens wave to-day. There are faces which nightly by the side of couches and in the flush of morning are lifted to heaven for me in prayer. They express all that the human heart may feel of love and solicitude for man. Yet in the face of Him who lifteth the light of His countenance upon me as I speak, I behold the expression of a love deeper, a tenderness more tender, a longing more intense, than ever heart of flesh might feel or human features express.

If all these voices should be hushed, all these faces averted, all these eyes turned away, the love of God for me would still remain unchanged and unchangeable. By the ministrations of it while I live shall I find all needed support, and at death be folded in its embrace forever.

The centuries seem rolled together as I speak, the past becomes the present, and out of the distance, like notes of music from afar, swelling into the distinctness of utterance as they roll, culminating over your heads in benediction, I catch once more the song that never dies, — "On earth peace, good-will toward men."

SERMON III.

THE RELATION OF BELIEF TO PRACTICE.

"Seest thou how faith wrought with his works, and by works was faith made perfect?" — JAMES ii. 22.

THE Apostle is here insisting on the value of works and their relation to faith. There is a certain earnestness and urgency in every line of this chapter which show that James was greatly wrought upon by his subject. He was evidently a very zealous worker himself, and thoroughly awake to the importance of Christian activity. What a rubbing of eyes and pricking up of ears there would be on the part of our drowsy church-members if the Apostle could visit Boston in the flesh, go down to North Street, and then stand in our pulpits and tell the churches what he had seen and heard, and what needed to be done in this Christian city! Of all the Apostles I do not think that I would surrender my pulpit to any of them so willingly as to James. No one can read this chapter and not feel that the writer was all aglow with the conviction that the churches were in imminent danger. There is a certain tinge of impatience, of moral indignation, running through these passages, as if they were in peril of falling into a fatal error as to what constituted Christian living, and he could not refrain from telling them of it. They were in danger, and the danger was this, — they were exaggerating the value of an intellectual belief. They were making religion to consist overmuch in mental conception and too little in practice. Christianity was becoming a matter of the head, and was being divorced from the hand and heart. James saw the danger, and threw himself across the path of declension and said to the churches, "You cannot go a rod farther in this direction unless you walk over my warning and my authority." Now I ask the thoughtful men and women in this audience if this is not precisely the peril to which the church is exposed to-day. The faith of the Evangelical churches is sound enough, the forms of belief are correct enough, but the actual working power of the churches is dangerously weak. Take a dozen or twenty persons out of every hundred of their membership, and what would become of the churches? The fact is, — and the sooner we look the fact squarely in the face the better it will be for Christ and us all, — the fact is, a small minority of the church do all the work that is being done in the church. Many of our religious organizations are like unused, reservoirs, into which the living water runs and then stagnates. The church in its internal structure is essentially the same that it was a hundred years ago. It ignores the difference between city and country life, between agricultural sections and great commercial centres, between the wants and opportunities of a small, thinly populated parish and the wants and necessities of a densely crowded metropolis. In its internal organization, in its power to give the public what it wants, the church is an anachronism. You might as well think that a hundred wells with the old-fashioned bucket and sweep could supply this city with water as that you can convert this city while your churches use only the same means of instruction and reform as were employed fifty years ago. The Young Men's Christian Associations are a standing protest against the blindness and slowness of the churches. They were formed by active Christian men, and are working outside the church because the church did not attempt the work inside itself. These bodies of young men are doing what the churches should have done. Twenty years ago every Evangelical church in Boston should have had a young men's Christian association in it. What a harvest might have been reaped for God, and where might correct doctrine have stood to-day, if the Orthodox churches had earned the gratitude of those young men who have flocked into this city for the last twenty years! Those young men, now middle-aged, own and control one half of Boston to-day. Error will never be headed off here by preaching and praying alone. When error represents intellect, when it represents philanthropy, when it represents art and culture and music, you must fight it with its own weapons. Match eloquence with eloquence, match culture with a higher finish, match its philanthropy with wider plans and a more generous outlay for human weal. Indolence can never overcome activity. Lethargy can never conquer wakefulness. Faith can never hold its own against works. No creed can be as beautiful as good deeds. The teaching and the feeding of the multitude must go together. A belief without any adequate expression in acts is like an organ, when all its pipes are silent and its keys untouched. It is dumb. It charms no one. It attracts no one. But bring forth the player; let him press the keys, let the dead air in all the choral columns be started into vibrations, and how the anthem swells, and how hearts are lifted on the waves of sound, and all the thousands applaud, some with their hands, others with eyes filled with happy tears. That which was dumb has spoken, and the multitude hasten to give it praise.

So it is with a creed. Write it out with whatever care you can; let it be perfect in its phraseology, skilful in its definitions, indisputable in its authority, this and nothing more, — and who cares for it? Does it touch any one's heart? Does it gain adherents? No. The world will never again fight over words as it once did. There will be no more church councils, like the Council of Trent, to last twenty years. Men are too busy nowadays to spend half a lifetime in debating theological dogmas. But bring forth a man who has a good creed which he expresses in acts, — let him say, "I love God with all my heart, and my neighbor as myself," and let him show it, — and men will point to him and say, "A religion which will make a man act as Mr. A. does is the religion for me." And so religion is honored by his conduct, and his creed gains adherents.

This, then, is what I wish to speak of to you this evening, — the relation of a creed, or a set form of belief, to practice; and I hope to show that a creed is influential, and influential for good upon the practice.

It is fashionable nowadays to say, "I don't care what a man thinks, if he only acts rightly." The better way to put it would be, "I don't care what a man thinks, if he don't act rightly." For a notoriously bad man has little influence in shaping public opinion, and hence he can do comparatively little mischief. But a good man has influence, and hence his every word becomes potential. There are two classes here in the community at the present time, both of which are in the wrong. The one class is composed of those who exalt the form of belief; loving and valuing creeds in themselves considered, disconnected from practice. They prize the church for the truths it holds, and not for the work it performs. Or, rather, they think that if the church is sound in the faith, if its doctrinal position is correct, if it holds to the form of sound words, — it is doing a great work, it is meeting the demands of the age; and they listen with impatience to any criticism which may be made of it. They are apt to resent any strictures upon their conduct as an impertinent, injudicious, and unwarrantable interference with what in their eyes is well enough as it is. Now, my friends, this position is all wrong. It is essentially the same position that James in his epistle to the churches so vigorously inveighed against. It is elevating faith above works. It is putting too much stress upon the form of belief, and too little upon its practical expressions. It not only divorces faith from works, but it arrays the two — which by nature are as closely allied as the spring and stream — against each other, thereby creating an antagonism which does not naturally exist. The value of a belief is measured by the same law as the value of a well. The question is, not how much it will hold, but how much it will yield; not solely as to the purity of the water or the amount of it, but the great point is, How much thirst can it quench? how many dying ones can it revive and save? This is what gives value to a belief; this is what makes Christianity so precious to man.

The second class who are in error is made up of those who say, "The belief is of no importance anyway. I do not care what a man thinks, if he only acts rightly." Well, friends, there is truth in that, and it is because there are some grains of truth in it that it is dangerous. The Devil never sends his sowers out with bags full of pure tare-seeds. He mingles a few dozen tare-seeds in a bushel of wheat, and so he gets his evil doctrines scattered and sown broadcast in the public mind, — scattered, too, by good men who suppose that they are sowing nothing but God's own truth all the while.

Now this is the portion of truth in the saying, "I don't care what a man thinks, if he only acts rightly," — namely, a mere sentiment over against an act weighs little. A man's opinion may affect only himself, but his acts affect society at large. A man may think it right to steal; but so long as he refrains from stealing, no one suffers but himself because of his opinion. A person may think it right to throw a railroad train off the track; but so long as he does not do it, the travelling public is not injured. On the other hand, a man may be kindly disposed and sympathetic in words and thoughts; but if he gives no material expression to his charity, who is the better for it? The Apostle puts this idea excellently in this illustration. It comes down nearer to the nineteenth-century style of speaking than almost any passage of Scripture.

"If a brother or sister be naked and destitute of daily food, and one of you say unto them, 'Depart in peace, be you warmed and filled'; notwithstanding ye give them not those things which are *needful to the body*, what doth it profit?"

So you see, if James was in the right of it, it is what a man actually does that meets the demands of duty and benefits society. And so far they speak truth who say, "It is what a man does, and not what he believes, that we care for." But the error lies in this, that this form of expression overlooks one great point, namely, the close connection which exists between believing and doing. It ignores the fact that back of every act and as its parent is a thought, and that the child is apt to be of the same character as the father. Man is a thinking and reasoning being. He acts from convictions, or from impulses which are the result of previous conviction; and hence it is that his conduct and his views have a very intimate relation to each other. It will not do to say, "I do not care what a man thinks," when in fact it is what a man thinks that decides how he will act. Going before and as the cause of every act is a positive mental decision, and every decision is the result of previous education and reflection. To say otherwise is to dethrone man and take the sceptre of self-sovereignty out of his hand. I want to make every young man in this audience feel that it makes a vast difference with his life and prospects what opinions he forms and what views he adopts; and hence it makes a vast difference what instructions and what instructors he has. I want to illustrate, on the level of every one's comprehension, that it makes a great difference what a man thinks, because of the influence which opinion has upon practice.

Take, for instance, one of your city police, to test the influence of one's views on his conduct, and the relation of the two. Suppose that a policeman should get it into his head that he is the best and most proper judge of guilt before the law. Suppose that he has a very poor opinion of courts and judges as agencies to administer law, (and I am not so sure that he would differ from many of us if he should.) Suppose he should say to himself, "I know what the law is, — where it is right and where it is wrong, where it oppresses and where it protects with a wise and needed protection, and I will administer it myself." He is conscientious in this, as I can conceive a police-officer might often be, and resolves himself into a judge and the station-house into a supreme court, and proceeds to adjudicate on every case that comes within his cognizance, — tries one, exonerates another, sends the third to prison, and hangs the fourth, — takes the entire administration of law into his own hands; — does it honestly, does it because he feels it to be the best thing for the city. What would you men say to it? What would the law-making and law-interpreting power say to such conduct? Say! They would say that such usurpation of undelegated authority strikes at the very root of all government. Nor would the justice of the officer's decision affect the matter at all. Crime might be the more swiftly and surely punished, but the evil of his conduct would remain the same. The virtue and efficiency of the man would tell all the deadlier against free institutions. A just tyrant is the worst of tyrants. So you see that it does make a difference what a man thinks, if he happens to be on the police force.

Or, again, take a merchant as an illustration. Let him be a man whose sole ambition is to amass wealth, who halts at nothing, provided it will bring him money, and not subject him to imprisonment. He laughs at honesty; ridicules integrity as an old-fashioned and obsolete idea; cheats and swindles and steals, only in such a way that the law cannot get its grip on him. Take such a man, — one of your prosperous villains, — and what is the effect of his life and practice? In the first place, I answer, such a man degrades business, and brings a stigma upon an otherwise honorable pursuit. He assists also to debauch public sentiment, and lower the tone of public morals. He gives to commercial life an ignoble object, and inspires young men, dazzled with his successful trickery, with a base ambition. He sets a bad example to every one of his clerks, to every young business man in the city; and thereby does much to make its business character bad, not merely for the present, but for the future. A man whose virtue is supported on one side by the fear of public opinion and by the terror of the jail on the other, who swindles honest men by "cornering" some railroad stock, and withholds from the government a portion of his taxable income, is a cheat and a public peril. Such a man, like any other nuisance, ought to be abolished. So you see that it makes a difference what a man believes if he happens to be a merchant.

Or, again, take a judge. Let him be a man indifferent as to justice, caring only for the salary and emolument of his office, unbraced by any nice sense of official obligation, — such a judge as some of our cities are cursed with, who sit like an incubus on the neck of our jurisprudence, strangling and loading it down with the weight of their iniquitous decisions so heavily that it can barely keep its feet and stagger along, — a judge who holds the balance in one hand, while the other is busy is taking bribes. Take such a judge, I say, and tell me if it does not make a difference what a man's views are; if it is so small a matter, after all, what opinion a man holds and what theory of legal administration he believes in?

Well, society is not composed solely of policemen and merchants and judges, but nearly every person exerts more or less influence upon it; and what is true of one is true of all, that what a man thinks decides in a great measure what a man does, and so it is of vast importance to the community that every member of it should have proper views and hold to proper opinions. By as much as men are ignorant and prejudiced, by as much as they have wrong views of government, by so much will their actions be wrong and their influence hurtful. And in nothing else is this so evident as in matters of religion; and upon no other thing is it so essential that the public should be rightly informed as concerning its views of God and those relations which spring from his control over us.

Now in this city, unfortunately, there exists a difference of opinion concerning some of the principal truths of revelation. I say that this is unfortunate; for both parties cannot be in the right, and therefore the influence of the one or the other class must be hurtful.

You may take the matter of the divinity of Christ. A majority of the city hold that Christ is divine, that is, truly God. A minority, on the other hand, respectable in point of numbers, and of considerable influence, hold that Christ was simply a human being; or rather (for there is great latitude of opinion among their own members), that He was a created being, and, being a creature, less than God. Some hold that He was purely and simply a man like Socrates or Plato or John Brown, while others maintain that He was a superior being, an angel, a prince among angels perhaps, but in no sense divine.

I am not to repeat before you to-night the evidences of Christ's divinity. I have not the time, nor does the object I have in view in this discourse require me to do it. I simply wish to make the statement, to show the difference of opinion between these two classes, and the difference that it must make in one's conduct whether a person thinks that Christ was God in the flesh or simply a man.

On the one hand, if He was simply a man, then the entire significance of the New Testament is changed from what it is if Christ is God; for it makes a great difference in my mind and yours, in my life and yours, whether the central figure which moves through all its history and gives its dignity to it, is God in human form, or a mere man, — simply one of the millions of the human race. When Christ speaks, it makes — and I cannot prevent it — a great difference, in my views of

Him, whether I regard His words as the utterance of the Deity Himself, or the expression of an individual opinion; when He says, alluding to God, "I and my Father are one," I must decide, in order to know what to think and do, whether it is the calm statement of conscious divinity, or nothing but the extravagant and blasphemous assertion of a Galilean peasant; and the influence of the New Testament on my life, in shaping my daily conduct, is largely decided by what I think of Christ. For, as all of you will admit, Christ is so intimately connected with it, He is so much the light and life of it, that my regard and reverence for it rises or sinks with my opinion of Him. He is the column around which all its history, its precepts, its doctrines, are twined; and with the fall of the central shaft all the pendent surroundings are cast in one tangled and disordered mass to the ground. If a man, then is the Sermon on the Mount no more to me than the dialogue of Socrates with his friends in the prison before he drank the fatal cup, or the speculations of Plato. If God, then is it the utterance of Heaven itself, and I regard it as the supreme expression vouchsafed to man for the government of his dispositions and the salvation of his soul.

Or, again, if Christ is God, then is He the fit object of prayer and worship, and my soul can go to Him as unto the ultimate object of its desires and adoration. If only a created being, then is it sin for me to address Him in prayer and praise; for we are solemnly forbidden to worship any but God alone.

My friends, be pleased to observe I am not arguing the matter. I am simply stating to you, impartially, certain facts, and deducing from them certain conclusions, to which I think all of you who are intelligent and candid must assent. And my point is to show, not what we should believe of Christ, but that it makes a great difference with ourselves and others what we do think. It is not a matter of little importance, but of the most solemn interest to every one of you, and not alone to you, but to all those, your children and friends, upon whom, by example and instruction, you have influence. And I hope none of you will ever say, "O, it don't make much difference what you think about Christ, if you only act rightly." For it does make a vast difference. First, because we should think of Him nothing but what is truth, neither adding to nor detracting from his dignity. And, secondly, because our action toward Him depends very much on what we think of Him.

Now, I wish to mention one other point of disagreement in public opinion here, concerning religious matters, in further illustration of my theme. It is this. There are those who say that, spiritually, men are not by nature very badly off, and that when the Bible insists on repentance and faith as the sole conditions of salvation, the expression is not to be taken literally. As men are not very bad by nature, they do not need a Saviour, and little anxiety need be felt about the matter any way.

Another class maintain that men by nature are very badly off; so badly that they are lost, that is, morally alienated from and opposed to God, through whose favor alone salvation can come. That a great change is needed, on the part of every soul, to fit it for heaven; that this change can be secured by accepting of certain terms published in the Gospels, and in no other way; and hence a most urgent duty rests upon every person to examine into the matter and make a positive decision.

Now there, in substance, are the two positions; there are the two beliefs. Suppose that they are held in equal sincerity, and observe the influence of each upon the believer.

This is one of those fortunate methods of investigation where the inquirer can reach a conclusion as accurate as a mathematical definition. You all see, at a glance, what is the legitimate effect of each of these beliefs upon the mind and heart.

The tendency of the first is to remove all anxiety from the mind concerning one's own spiritual condition, or that of others, and lessen to a corresponding extent the motive to act. For no one will warn or entreat another, unless he is persuaded there is peril ahead. And it is the law, both of self-preservation and solicitude for others, that the effort put forth is commensurate with the felt imminence of the danger.

The legitimate result of the other belief upon the mind is to deepen the impression of danger, provoke investigation, and elicit effort. And here, too, as the belief is sincerely held and the awful truth in its fulness apprehended, will the effort tally with the conviction. All missionary effort now being put forth in the world, all personal solicitude felt for friends, is inspired by this motive, — to save men from a threatening peril. There is not a prayer uttered, there is not a petition sent up to Heaven's throne, there is not an anxiety felt, there is not a loving endeavor made, for man's conversion that has not this fear, this belief, for its parent and source. This, too, is the origin of that sublime motive which keeps the gospel ministry full of faithful laborers. Back of me, ever, as I speak to you, as a vast energy pushing me ever on, and holding me ever up, is the thought that many of you are in danger of living and dying unreconciled to God; and that I am set to warn and persuade you, and bring you penitent and rejoicing to our common and loving Father's presence. Do you think that any young man of capacity — which always carries with it ambition —

would deny himself the honors, the possible wealth, and, what is stronger yet with men, the keen exhilaration of secular life, and devote himself to teaching men the way of salvation, unless he felt that men were in danger, — a danger from which he might possibly save them?

My friends, it is because I believe that many of you are in peril that I am here to-night. It was the conviction that men were morally wrong by nature, and liable to make an eternal wreck of themselves, and that I might possibly, by God's aid, save some of them, that I put my foot on the dream of my life, and entered a profession which was by no means my first choice. It is this thought and hope which hold me to-day in a position which, left to my own inclination, I would that any other man filled. I dare to say that many a young man in the ministry wishes that he was pastor of a city church, and is planning for the day when he shall be. He knows nothing of what he desires. A city life, as many of you by dire experience know, is a grinding kind of a life. It grinds the hope and life and vigor out of a man. It wrinkles the face, and whitens the head, and puts burdens upon men beyond what flesh and blood can bear. It taps and exhausts all the reserved forces of one's nature. It destroys all individuality, and makes a man to be no more than one ant amid countless numbers of its kind. And there are few of you here who are under its influence, who feel the cruel and pitiless friction of its ponderous and ever-revolving pressure settling with every year more heavily upon you as it revolves, but that long for the quiet and rest, the healthy toil, the broad scope and free air, of the country. And were it not for the duties and responsibilities which bind us here, many of us would break away and escape forever from what we feel is slowly but surely killing us. The duty which brought and keeps me here is born of this thought, I say, that many in this city are morally in a wrong position, and that I must go as a brother, prompted by love, to tell them of their danger. I fear that many of you in this audience are not spiritually right and at peace with God; your lives are not such lives as you might live, and as you ought to live, and I am here to tell you of it, and warn you of a danger you do not see. My friends, there are gales on the ocean, and your ships are not prepared for storm. You are blind to the lightning and deaf to the angry mutterings of the thunder. The heavens are black over your heads, and the swell of a coming tempest begins to make itself felt in your fears, and I charge you to-night to seek the help of Him who alone can walk the waters you soon must sail, who alone can break the bank which rolls up toward you black and heavy with destruction, and scatter it in golden mist. There is but one safe pilot on the river of death: he is Christ. There is but one voice able to say to the elements which threaten to engulf you, "Peace, be still!" It is the voice of Him who of old rebuked the Galilean surge. He who preaches salvation to men who cannot be lost stultifies his intelligence, and spends his life for naught.

I have thus from several directions brought you down to a common conclusion, and you all see and say with me that it does make a vast difference what a man believes. It makes a difference with a police-officer, and with the merchant, and with the judge, and with the preacher; for it decides what his conduct and teaching shall be. Back of all loose practice, and as a parent of it, you will find, by searching, a loose opinion What we think is a spur to what we shall do, and all action is but the result of previous decision.

Were this not true, of what value would education be? What would it matter whether we were educated rightly or wrongly? Of what use would the mind itself be? Why carry so costly a pilot as reason, if it matters not whether we steer this way or that?

Here in our midst is a mighty force moving us as the wind moves the ship, and according to the direction and force of it are we blown to favor and fortune or the reverse. We call it public opinion.

It is mightier than law; for it can take the strongest and best law ever enacted, and make it of no more account than a piece of parchment, that a child can tear with its fingers and cast to the winds. It is mightier than governments; for it can level thrones and change constitutions. It is mightier than all armies; for it speaks, and at its word armies melt away, — one returning to his shop, another to his farm, and another to his merchandise. Yea, it is mightier than the church itself; for creeds and covenants yield to its touch, and orders, sacred with the sanction of centuries, at its command yield their existence and pass forever away. But what is public opinion, and of what is its mighty energy composed? It is made up, my friend, in part of what you and I think. There is not a vibration in the air but that can contribute something to the hurricane, and make its rush fiercer and its roar more to be dreaded. There is not a single beam of all the myriads that the sun sends out that does not increase our comfort, and make the earth healthier and happier. And so there is not a thought of our minds, there is not a dream of our life, there is not a word of our lips, which does not enter that vast volume of power called public opinion, — enter to make it stronger for good or for evil. It is a question of public importance, therefore, what you and I believe. It affects society and the world at large.

It affects men's lives here and their destiny hereafter, what we think of the Bible and of Christ, who in it is called the Lord and Saviour of all. I wish you to understand, therefore, that, in the long run, neither your own acts nor the acts of those whom you influence will be better in character than your thoughts. If you are mean and bigoted and envious and spiteful in your thoughts of men, you will very likely be the same in your acts toward them. If you are a business-man, and dishonest in trade, you are educating all your clerks in dishonesty, and doing all you can to degrade and debauch business in this city, and people it with dishonest tradesmen ten years from now. You are not only giving a bad character to the city to-day, but deciding that it shall continue bad. And now what need I say further? You came here to be taught and quickened in mind and heart, and I have done what I might to help you touching the matter discussed. The pleasantest thought of my ministry here is, that you who make up my audience from evening to evening do not come to sleep, but to think, — that mind and heart and enterprise have here an audience. I dare say that some of you do not always agree with me, and that you who do not are sometimes in the right; but this does not stir a ripple of fear as to the result. For the more men who are striving to grow in the understanding of every duty, and to get at the root of things,—the more such men think and investigate, the nearer will they come together; for truth is a fixed point, and all who seek it—no matter how widely they be apart—must inevitably converge. The people who butt against each other are those who run about blindfold.

And now, friends, you who are of like theological opinions with myself, know this, that the great lesson for us to learn is, how to express more of Christian spirit in our acts. We are to let the world, we are to let this city, see, not what our faith is, nor what our works are, but how our faith works with our works, and is to them what the sun is to the rose,—the source of its color and fragrance. I am convinced more and more that it is not by logic and argument and verbal demonstration that Christ is to be set forth to the intellect and heart and conscience of this city. Nor by denunciation and pharisaical isolation can ignorance be enlightened and enmity converted to friendship. We must raise the level of our lives; we must widen and deepen the channel of sympathy for man; we must so act that Christ shall have, as it were, a second incarnation in our own persons,—or ever that banner, which is white as an angel's wing, lifted by universal suffrage here, shall wave unchallenged over all. If evangelical doctrines are better than other doctrines, then should the lives of those who hold them be better, their charity wider, their love for man warmer, their zeal greater, and their acts, more than the acts of other men, like His to whom they claim to have come nearer in the understanding of His truth. To this test, I warn you, evangelical religion must eventually come for measurement. In this balance, before its adherents and opponents, I confess to-night it is just that it shall be weighed. For the resources of statement were exhausted centuries ago when Christ declared, "By their fruits ye shall know them."

Here and with this plummet, then, we at last touch bottom. Before such a demonstration of the value of our belief error could not live. So far as it was honest, it would be converted; so far as it was only cunning and wickedness, it would be detected and despised. Let that religion which is the quickest to feed the hungry, to clothe the naked, to enlighten ignorance, to lift the fallen, to cheer the hopeless, — and which has the most charity toward its enemies, be the future religion of this city. Write it over the doors of all your churches in characters that shall never fade; print it as the caption of every profession of faith; teach it to your children; proclaim it to the winds, and charge them to bear it to every land, — that hereafter in this city he who loveth man the best is the truest disciple of Christ, and the best representative of God. Let this be our creed; and we invoke this as the final test, in the years ahead, of our faith.

SERMON IV.

TO YOUNG MEN.

"I have written unto you, young men, because ye are strong, and the word of God abideth in you, and ye have overcome the wicked one." — 1 JOHN ii. 14.

THE idea of strength is intimately connected with youth. Age is the synonyme of weakness, — at least, of diminished vigor. The human frame with its once hardy flesh and swelling sinews shrunk and shrivelled, the erectness of its stature gone, the lustreless eye, the tremulous hand, the unsteady knees, — these speak of vigor departed, of motion checked, of beauty fled. They suggest the settling of the current, and the ebbing of the vital powers.

But youth is strong. Neither weakness nor decay belong to it. It is full of growth and facile movements. Observe a grove of trees when in green, luxuriant prime. How lithe and flexile! With trunk sunk like a firmly set pillar deeply in earth, braced and fastened by a hundred lateral and far-reaching supports, and with branches whose beginnings are in its very heart, stretching wide out on either side, pliant and tough, each tree, with tossing top and streaming foliage, stands against the blast tremulous with delight, and laughing defiance at the wind. What cares such a tree for the gale? It meets it like a broad-chested man, inhaling new life and vigor from its violence, and tosses its flexile branches against it in disdain. How often we have all seen such trees, and sat and watched them sway and bend, stoop and rise, while every leaf stood out straight as a streaming flag! Such trees type the qualities and characteristics of youth.

Take a young man inured to toil, — I do not mean a slim, fragile lad, such as are nestled in babyhood in the suffocating down of your cities, but such as were rocked on the hard oaken floor of the country, — broad in the chest, with shoulders thick and square. Bare his breast and neck. What breadth, what fulness! See how the blue veins cross it, taut with healthy blood! Turn his head, and observe how with the motion the great ridges of the well-twisted cords come out. Lift the arm; move it up and down in the socket, and mark the play of the tough sinews. Watch the face with its broad brow, the keen, lively eyes, the crisp beard, the wide, squarely set jaw. Who has ever looked on such a piece of God's creative power, and not marvelled? And who of us, with such a picture in our mind, wonders that the Apostle should say, "I have written unto you, young men, because ye are strong"?

Well, this idea of strength, of capacity, suggests

the sequent idea of responsibility. For youth is not sluggish, nor is its strength unexercised. But no one puts forth strength, — no one whose life has a river-like motion to it, — but incurs responsibility. A life which flows through society, sweeping all before it, lifting everything up on it, is something to watch and direct aright. It is easy to imagine that John had this in mind when he wrote this Epistle, and said, "I have written unto you, young men, because ye are strong," active, and hence responsible.

Perhaps, generally speaking, the thought of his responsibility is not the uppermost one in a young man's mind, as he plunges into the bustle and excitement of an active life. Fame, wealth, personal appearance, how he can best enjoy himself, — these and the like are the thoughts which fill his mind and inspire him with motive power. He looks upon the present, with all its richly tinted clusters of sensuous pleasure, as free to his hand, and that he has a perfect right to seize and drain them into his cup. Of the remote influence of his action, either upon himself or others, he rarely, if ever, thinks. He forgets, or does not wish to remember, the effect of his conduct and example for good or evil upon the community; but such thoughtlessness, such forgetfulness of moral obligation, is cognizable by justice. God never framed one law of responsibility for the old and another for the young; and never are men so responsible, never are they so worthy or unworthy, never so royally justified or so fearfully condemned, as when their brains are the most active, their bodies the strongest, and the current of their life at its fullest flood and flow.

Now, this idea of responsibility is not calculated when rightly considered, to fetter and gag a man, and does not. He who feels it, having conceived of it rightly, energizes none the less, and laughs none the less. And I am never more vexed than at the views hypochondriacal people have upon this point. There is too much of this feeling extant, that the eye of God is on a man just to ascertain when he can punish. God is a kind and loving father, acting on the level of our sonship with Him in Christ, and not a keen-eyed, heartless overseer, standing over us whip in hand, goading us to unpaid toil, and finding joy in our looks of fear and terror. It is a crying shame that in the full, mellow light of the Gospel, which has warmed the earth with a genial and fructifying warmth these two thousand years, men and women should be found lashing themselves like mediæval monks, and talking as if penance is piety, and slavish self-denial discipleship. Nothing so favors self-righteousness as the opinion that severe regimen and mean clothes and pharisaical exactness give evidence of adoption. These folks will find, in the great hour of transition, that it was Christ's blood, and not their severe morality, their crabbed and unamiable strictness, that saved them. I often think that some good people I know will fancy for a moment, after they have been wafted into the singing and jubilant throngs, that the upbearing and attendant angels have dropped them a little too soon and in the wrong spot, so happy and cheerful will the faces around them be. And what if the harps should have a livelier tone, and the jubilant hands less solemnity of gesture, than accorded with their notion of heavenly action on earth!

No, the love of God toward us, my friends, is not a kind of severe charity, breaking the bread of his bounty only to the deserving and to those whose lives are cut after the strictest regulation pattern; but a warm, genial sentiment, rather, feeding without question and without rebuke all the hungry and the faint who will accept of its blessed provision; yea, casting far and near on the waters of life that bread which, if once eaten, forbids further hunger forever.

Revelation is not the only fountain out of which the waters of His healing flow, and in which His face and form are mirrored. Nature, in other colors, and from a less palpable negative, prints Him to the eye. The flowers and grasses, the stars, and every lovely sight and sweet smell we see or inhale, are of Him. In them you see the Divine nature working itself out in all manner of beautiful colors and forms, — the same nature that gave us in compassion Christ, and yearns to-night, beyond the yearning of a dying wife for her absent husband, over every erring sinner in this audience or in the world.

Be it remembered, then, that the responsibility which a young man incurs by his every word and act, be it never so grave, is not a feeling to repress him. The requirements of God are not like so many withes bound tightly around the limbs, congealing the blood and benumbing the senses. The grace of God enlarges every part of a man, as moisture and warmth do a tree. A Christian not only grows in the fulfilment of duty, but in the enjoyment of it as well. He is not only taught how to touch one string and call forth one note, but he sweeps the cords of a harp whose strings are multitudinous, and whose ever-growing volume and richness of tone are a daily surprise to him. His conscience is not only rendered more acute, but his susceptibilities of enjoyment are more keen and abundant. Grace acts on the soul, as water on a sponge. It puts it into a condition to absorb and take in more than before it was thus moistened and made yielding. Hence it is that a man feels more and better, acts more and better, has larger hopes and keener joys, is more companionable, charitable, and generous, as he grows heavenward. Thus it comes about, in the case of young men, that God does not seek to check the strong tides of feeling which throb and swell in their veins. He welcomes them, as the miller hails with joy the rush and roar of torrents in the hills above. The aspirations of youth, the ambition of early manhood, are the very waters with which he drives the wheels of a thousand activities, and sets a thousand spindles in motion. God does not want stagnation, but movement, impulse, action, the whir of wheels and the whiz of belts, by the well-directed force of which the woof and web of His formative providence are growing day by day.

But while this idea of responsibility should not repress a man, should not fetter or gag him, it should quicken him to great caution and care. It is with a man as with a horse. Speed, vigor, fire, while they enhance his value, call for the exercise of great watchfulness on the part of the driver. Blood and spirit are excellent in a horse; but it needs a taut line, a strong bit, and a steady hand to guide such. But, in spite of this, who, with any sense of judgment, any appreciation of noble qualities, would choose an old, rickety, shambling hack in preference to a deep-chested, strongly hipped roadster, that will go swinging along at the rate of twelve miles to the hour without tiring, —

or a gay, foxy-looking animal, with the blood of the desert coursing beneath his velvet hide, and with a motion so swift and a look so spirited, that as you watch him you say with delight, "The old fable is true,—that horse was born of the wind and the sunshine." And so it is in the case of young men. Away with your dull, sluggish, and inert natures, that are content to doze life away in the same narrow sphere their fathers filled, and who bring out in all their living nothing higher or more noble than a poor repetition of the past!

If there is one thing which Christianity favors more than all else, it is this, — future improvement on what has been. In the Scripture doctrine of the millennium human effort finds its highest incitement and human progress its amplest vindication. From this doctrine, alike applicable to every age, as from an unfailing cruse, the lamps which have lighted men forward have ever been filled. The fact that there is to be a state of morals purer than the world has yet reached, and a state of culture higher than the mind has yet achieved, proves that we must go on. By this sublime prediction, man, whether willing or unwilling, is pushed, as with the hand of a giant, to greater things than he has yet attained. The beautiful thing about Christianity is that it improves the individual man. It elevates the masses through the dissemination of personal virtues. It begins with one man and in one heart, and reforms it, and then multiplies this one result into thousands by the same process. The human race — each contaminated soul in it, made to be the temple of the Holy Ghost — is to be renovated, as houses are in an infected city, one by one. Religion means the cleansing of what now is soiled, the straightening of what now is crooked, the widening of what is narrow and cramped. It means progress, development, invention. Now every young man should keep this in mind. He should forget what is behind, and reach forward to that which is ahead. The past is dark, sombre, unsatisfactory, — like a bank of clouds silvery as to its upper edges, and crossed here and there with lanes of crimson; but, on the whole, suggestive of cheerless fogs and chilling rain. The future, like a clear azure-tinted sky, such as a golden sunset gives us after a day of storm, illuminated from unseen sources, with its enlarged activities, its ever-widening possibilities, in which Christ is to stand in the majesty of a universal and a universally acknowledged sovereignty, is what should inspire and constrain you. No young man should be content to be as his father is. We have never had moral forces enough in the world to convert the world. That, at least, is certain. The millennium will never be reached by a reproduction of what has been. He should be wiser and better than his father. He should know more of God and do more for man. He should stand one grade higher, in all that ennobles character, than any of his name who have gone before him. Over this road, wide as hope itself, and macadamized with promises of the Most High, the generations of the future are to march until they shall come to that city whose maker and builder is God, whose walls are salvation and whose Gates are praise.

I know that occasionally you hear some bemoaning the present, and growling out dissatisfaction with everything modern. Owlish by nature, they perch themselves above ruins, and croak their dismal cries over departed greatness. To such, the age which has seen more conversions to Christ than any preceding is the most wicked, and the fifty years that have built more schoolhouses and colleges than half as many centuries before are the years in which wisdom and virtue have been rapidly declining. But who cares for such croakers? If the owl and the bat can tolerate them, we can. We know that their predictions are only such as the graves have ever made to the cradles. God's providence never halts, never retires. Railroads and the telegraph have not backed us into the Dark Ages. Free schools and free Bibles and free governments are not so many clean victories for the Devil. As the rods which Agassiz planted at the foot of the glacier, and which he found on his return had blossomed, revealed how far the icy mass had receded, so our progressive enterprises and institutions, the rods which God has struck into this age, reveal how fast and how far the ponderous mass of ignorance and superstition has melted and is melting away under the potent influence of the Gospels.

Say, then, young men, knowing that you speak on the reliable basis of facts, say to all these shrivelled, mummified specimens of despondency, "Croak as you please; refuse to see if you will that the skies are bright and the grasses green; shut your eyes to the Godlike upward tendencies in man, which, inspired and strengthened by faith in Christ, are lifting the race heavenward: yet never was there an age so rich in the realizations of that hope which is an anchor, so blessed in the actual possession of liberty, or so auspicious with promise touching the future, as this in which you live and in which you ought to rejoice."

The very earnest repetition by the Apostle of this same idea emphasizes his solicitude for that portion of the church included in the phrase "young men." One reason of his anxiety may be found in the fact that this class is a very important one to the Church. From it she draws her teachers, and though her servants age and die, the ministry is always full. It is on young men also that she most relies to push her benevolent enterprises among the unregenerate and ungodly, and to conduct the more active canvassing incidental to seasons of great religious awakening. A church without a corps of efficient young men in it is like a tree without branches, or a ship without sails. But, on the other hand, let no one suppose — as some, I fear, do — that this class can meet all the requirements of a religious organization. The older are as necessary for the proper administration of affairs as the younger members. To continue the preceding figure, the aged are to the church and to the younger members themselves what the trunk is to the branches. They give to the organization stability, dignity, strength; and if the fruit is found upon the outlying branches, is it not because the parent trunk kindly sends the vitalizing sap out to them? The fact is, these two classes should work in loving and helpful conjunction. Any divorcement in acts or sympathy is unwarranted and hazardous. Any organization in which the two are not joined labors at a vast disadvantage. Spiritual forces depend in part on experience and character, and these do not come to one in a day. No church, for instance, can afford to dispense with the prayers of the more aged of her membership. There is a certain reach of thought, a certain profound apprehension of God's mercy and of human need, which seems to come only to the weakened and those who feel that they are nigh to their graves. In ancient times and in certain countries no man could ask a favor of his monarch until he could show a scar; and nothing so lifts one up as to hear a battle-scarred veteran of God plead for favors in the presence of his king. Each word goes up as the cry of one hard pressed before and behind with foes. It is the voice of one who, feeling that he stands on a treacherous element, cries, "Help, Lord, or I sink." Young Christians never get that cry, and never can, until time, and trouble, and conflict with the adversary have revealed his mightiness and their frailty.

There is another thought which aids us to estimate the value of young men to the church, and reveals why, like John, we should feel solicitous concerning them. It is this, — they keep the church progressive, and thus make it attractive to the masses, thereby adding to its efficiency. Let it be remembered that the race has risen in improvement, not as a man is lifted bodily by pulleys, but as one mounts a ladder, step by step, one round at a time. Now each generation is such a round. The world, in its progress upward, stands for a moment upon one, and is upheld by it, and then passes up and puts its weight on the next above. By this order of growth, the hope of the world is ever kept buoyant, its sympathies deep, and its faith active; for it is perpetually renewing its youth. In this law of growth the Church especially shares. She must share in it, or else come to a dead stand. Go back to her origin, and recall her history. The Church, as organized in Christ, was not an army of defence, for she had nothing to defend, but an army of invasion recruited for the express purpose of attack and capture. Her banners are not such as float over the walls of a citadel or an intrenched camp, but, rather, such as, held in bravely uplifted hands, stream fluttering out along the line of battle and above the heads of charging columns, crowding to death or victory. This fact it is which reveals why a bold, wide-awake, progressive church is so effective in its influence upon the world. Great success does not surprise such a church. Plans based upon the expectation of such success do not appall it. It provides accommodation ahead of its present wants and the wants of the public. It heightens and lengthens its dam, that no unused water escape. It adds wheel to wheel and stone to stone, that no water lie stagnant in the meadows above; and even then, not content, still eager, filled with divine expectation, it looketh continually unto the hills from whence cometh its strength for fresh and fuller outpourings of power-bestowing grace. Would that we had more such churches! I fear that nothing would surprise some of our churches so much as a revival. Should the heaven open, and the wind-like Spirit of God come down upon them in power, it would take, in their astonishment the very breath out of their bodies!

Now, friends, in an earnest, progressive church, young men always are, and must, from the very nature of things, be prominent. Any attempt at repression against this class on the part of the office-bearers of the church, any policy or management that shall alienate it, is as if a man should extract the blood-supplying elements from his food and expect to live. Such management, such administration of affairs, whether the managers realize it or not, no matter how honest the motive, is simply church suicide. It speedily becomes a poor, withered, and fruitless thing. The Church in her aspirations, in liberality of opinion, in charity of judgment, in soul and body saving activity, must be kept in the van of the age. If you would direct a stream, you must channel ahead of it, and not attempt to log up with obstructions its irresistible flow. The more orthodox a church is, the more wide-awake and progressive it should be, — the more ballast, the more sail. The more stanchly it adheres to essentials, the more liberal it should be in respect to non-essentials. A church need not fear any amount of lateral swinging and swaying so long as the anchor of its faith is struck deep into the Rock Christ Jesus. Heterodoxy has won nearly all her triumphs on side issues and by that greatest blunder of Orthodoxy, — its stand-still-and-do-nothingism. She has filled her granaries from fields we should have reaped, and out of the quarries we should have worked for the Lord she has hewn the material for her structure.

Now, the value of this young element in the church is that it will prevent this blunder from being repeated. The man who stumbles twice at the same stone, says the Spanish proverb, is a fool. The future will not be as the past. No more pointing at ships and saying, "See! ours are the best, the only well-ballasted ships in the harbor." Reeve in the sails, call your crews aboard, spread the canvas of every activity, and sail out upon the broad ocean of opportunity which stretches away beyond all voyaging of human thought, carrying such blessings to every part that gratitude shall belt the world with your praise. The future will do more than repeat the past. Orthodoxy, strong as white-oak and pliant as mountain-ash, shall be so interpreted as to be understood, and therefore loved, by the masses. Into the fibrous and plaited base of her wreath, woven from her doctrines, leaves many-colored, and flowers not a few nor lacking fragrance, shall be placed, and her garland shall be worthy the forehead of that system of salvation which has for its parents both the justice and the love of God. No longer dogmatic, no longer uncouth, tolerant hereafter toward everything but sin, no longer repellant, she shall adorn herself with the choicest culture, attracting the multitudes by her honesty on the one hand and the grace of her appearance on the other. No longer behind the age, filled with the spirit of progress, she shall light the race down the ages with the two orbs of her faith both luminous and at full glow, — love toward God and equal love toward all men. And the realization of that high hope to the Orthodox Church, founded in this country, through the agency of our fathers, by God Himself, is to come, more than from any other source, through the action of the young men today in the church.

As a further reason to warrant solicitude for young men, we might mention the intimate relation they must sustain to the future character and opportunities of the Church.

It is evident that the Church has reached that point at which her grandest and final triumphs are to be won. She stands upon the threshold of a future ablaze with the illuminations of victory. Upon the generation now coming into power God imposes such obligations as no preceding one was ever honored with. I say honored with, for the responsibilities which are of God spring from enlarged possibilities of usefulness. The character of that piety and virtue exhibited by the young men of the Church for the next thirty years will largely decide what its piety shall be for the next three hundred years. God has given it to our hands to sketch the outline of that typical Godliness into which the world is to grow as into the very stature of Christ. I pray you, young men, let that piety in you which is to type the piety of the future be measured by the utmost demand of Gospel requirement. Feel as though in your lives day by day you were laying the foundations of that temple the cap-stone of which centuries hence the happy, because redeemed, nations shall come together and lay with shoutings. Live so that from that remote age he who is chosen to express the thought of the multitude will point his finger to your graves and say, "The men and women who sleep there began what we to-day finish, and gave, through their lives, the first perfect expression of that piety which at last, as our eyes behold, has made the whole earth one."

To this end, gauge the opposition, that you may be stimulated to the requisite effort. Remember that your feet stand amid snares and on the edge of pitfalls. Remember that low piety in you means low piety wherever your example and influence extends. Your fall is not disastrous to you alone. It is equally, perhaps more fatal, to all whom your fall discourages and drags down with you. No life to-day is single or isolated.

Life is manifold and complex. It is intermingled, woven in and woven out, with other lives. As a transverse thread in the woof brings, by its irruption or fracture, looseness and severance to the entire piece, so the lapse of any man from virtue entails weakness and loss to the entire social and moral structure of which he is a part. Be steadfast, therefore, and watch unto prayer.

The Apostle writes unto young men, because, as he says, they are strong. But when is a young man strong? Is he strong when he is held and shaken like a very reed in the clutch of some base appetite? Is he strong when he is scourged and driven at the hand of some lust like a slave, and like a slave submits without shame or resistance? Is he strong when a low-bred sneer, a stinging taunt, or a silly banter can sheer him from a noble purpose? Is he strong when the breath of a woman expressed in an invitation to taste the wine-cup can blow his resolution and pledge into the air, and whirl them, as the wind whirls a feather, out of sight and thought? Is he strong when he is too cowardly to stand by his convictions of loyalty to Christ and virtue? No, a thousand times *no!* such a young man is not strong. If there is any such young man here to-night, within the sound of my voice, high or low, rich or poor, let this judgment come to you. I cast it at your conscience as men shoot flaming arrows into caverns to light up their horrible darkness. You are weak, — weak as a cord of flax in the blaze of a candle, or as last year's reeds on the banks of a river. John did not write to such as you. He wrote to young men who were strong, evidenced by the fact that they had " overcome the Wicked One."

Now that is a wonderful statement. And yet it is true in the case of every young man who has broken away from Satan and joined himself to Christ. Such a person has won a great victory. He never will know how great it is until from heaven, with holy and instructed vision, he contemplates the doings of Him who " spoiled principalities and powers, making a boast of them openly." To overcome Satan is to get the mastery over one who shook the thrones of heaven with jarring strife, and into this earth brought, even when weakened by defeat, sin and death. Marvellous conflict ! transcendent triumph ! a struggle which sets us forever free, and closes an unaccountable rebellion with an unending peace !

But this victory won by man is not of man. God nerves the arm that deals the blow, else powerless. The dead come forth, but only at the quickening word of Christ. This is a great mystery, — how man is free and God supreme, how we can strike and He do all the cutting. But what is hidden will by and by be plain. The fog will lift, and we shall see what current drifts our boat. Young birds are always dim of sight until their wings are plumed for upper air.

But though overcome, still the "wicked one" does not give up the contest, else a Christian's life would be fruition and not warfare, and we should all sit on thrones and not be running in the dust and heat of the race-course. The principle of evil has a sort of ugly immortality. In it lurks a subtle and deathless element. Diabolism is abused divinity. So it comes about that the Christian is always winning, yet always fighting. He conquers, and is always attacked; victorious, yet never at peace.

Now, young men, I take it that this is the case with us. We did once, each of us, with the Spirit's aid, wrestle so stoutly as to overcome the adversary. Yea, we got him down and had our knee on his breast and our grip on his throat, and we bore so hard on him that he lay powerless, and we thought that the life had gone out of him, and that we should be no more troubled by him forever. But scarcely had we risen and turned to go our way, when lo! our adversary stood before us as desperate, if not as strong, as ever. And so it is in the experience of all. A man can barely rise in the morning before he is set upon and must lock in for a close hug with his stout-backed foe. And many a bruise and painful fall have we all gotten in these rough encounters. And it behooves us all to make ourselves expert in the modes of spiritual attack and defence, to "prove every spirit," and be as wise as wrestlers, who study how to trip and recover and cast in their brave frolics.

Now, one thing that all young men need, and which God expects you to exhibit in this warfare, is high, undaunted resolution, — or, to put it in Saxon, *grit.*

To live uprightly and purely in this age is no play. A young man who resolves to do it must put himself, as a fencer does when about to be attacked, on his guard. He needs an eye like a swallow's, and a wrist pliant and well nerved, to parry the thrusts and ward off the passes of his foe. A mild and dove-like disposition does not hold a man up to the line of duty at all times. There are the mild, and there are also the heroic virtues of Christianity, and both find their proper moments of expression. There are times when a young man must say *no,* and bring it out like the snap of a frosty file. There are times also when he must say yes, and make it ring like the blast of a trumpet. Never did young men need this quality and temper more than they do to-day; never were there more opportunities for its exercise. Old issues are passing away, new ones are rising into view. In politics everything is chaotic, and a

Christian must pick his way by the exercise of his own conscience and judgment. God has given to this generation the rare privilege of changing its course without mortification, and its suffrage without inconsistency. He has made the line between right and wrong, between temperance and drunkenness, broader and clearer than ever before in the history of the world. No eye can fail to see it; and no confusing of issues, no partisan jugglery, no evasion of duty, can ever wipe it out. At your feet it is drawn, and there it will continue ineffaceable and well defined, until your position at the last assize shall be decided by your relation to it.

In social life the same is true. In parlors, and saloons, and on festive occasions, you will more than once be challenged by the tempter, and must needs bear witness for temperance and piety. At such supreme moments I entreat you not to flinch. Avoid rudeness, but never surrender principle. Never be so deceived by the sweetness of the draught as to swallow poison. Harmonize with no fashionable folly. Be not moved by sneers, nor swayed by banter, nor captured by entreaty. Be true to your highest conceptions of right, to those views of duty given in the Bible to man, and to those aspirations for holiness which come to you in moments of supreme moral elevation.

To conclude, I would say, — and I would say it personally to each one of you, — if you have ever yielded to temptation, ever stifled conviction, ever acted counter to your sense of right, ever been influenced by ridicule, ever joined in with less scrupulous companions, you did a weak, a wicked, and a silly thing. Never, so long as you draw breath, so misdemean yourself again. Live, henceforth, so near the Deity, by faith in Christ and along the line of correct conduct, that, in the hour of your supremest trial, you shall not only be justified, but also glorified, in the presence of God and those most holy angels of His, among whom as with fellow-servants you shall thenceforth live and love and adore forever.

SERMON V.

BURDEN-BEARING.

"For every man shall bear his own burden." — GALATIANS vi. 5.

IF you look at the second verse of this chapter, you will find these words, "Bear ye one another's burdens, and so fulfil the law of Christ," while our text asserts that every man shall bear his own burden. These two passages, standing in such juxtaposition and apparently contradictory, were once inexplicable to me. I found in one a command to bear another man's burden, and then, immediately following it, the assertion that every man should bear his own. How I could bear a person's burden if he was compelled to bear it himself, I could not understand. But that experience which years and trials bring to us all has interpreted these two passages correctly to me, and harmonized what formerly was discordant. I see now how it comes about that all of you can aid me in bearing my burden, and yet how, in spite of all your well-meant and needed assistance, I must bear my own burden.

I have not the time to amplify both of these passages, and thereby show you just where they connect, — just where the two statements blend into one, and give full expression to one and the same truth. But this, in passing, I will say, that there are some truths which you cannot express in a sentence : you cannot condense them into a passage; you cannot bring their legitimate pressure to bear upon the conscience in a single injunction.

When God, therefore, wishes to express any great truth, — which is but another way of saying when he wishes to express Himself, — He is compelled, as it were, to put it in more than one form of words. Truth is spherical, truth is cone-like, and the mind must encompass it in order to understand it. Thus it is with the Scriptures. In one passage God gives us one view of a truth, further on another, and yet further a third ; and so, by presenting it to us from many points of view, calling our attention to this and that side of it, He makes us at last understand it in its full force and completeness.

Moreover, He uses our experience to advance our understanding. One day reveals what the day before was hidden. There are many things in God's government over us which we did not comprehend once, but which we do comprehend now. There are questions in ethics, there are problems of body and mind, which were once mysterious, but which are now plain. From the tangled skein of our ignorance and misgiving each day's experience has unravelled some strand. With some of you the process is nearly completed, and the mass nearly threaded out.

Now in these two passages the main topic, the central shaft, is burden-bearing. This is the truth which, like a column written all over with hieroglyphs, we are to study. "Bear ye one another's burdens." That is one side of it. That teaches us the duty of sympathy, of tenderness, of mutual helpfulness. But come round to the side of our text, "For every man shall bear his own burden," and you see the other side, and the letters spell a different injunction.

Now I wish to show you, this evening, what burdens every man must bear for himself, and why and in what manner he is strengthened to bear them.

This, then, is my first proposition, namely, that every one must bear the burden of his own sins, both as concerns this life and the next.

The results of sin are strictly individual. It is with the soul as with the body, with the spirit as with the flesh. If you thrust a knife into your arm, it does not affect me. You yourself feel the pain; you yourself must endure the agony. I may sympathize, I may pity, I may bandage the gash, but the severed flesh and the lacerated fibres are yours, and along your nerves nature telegraphs the pain. So it is with the soul. A man who stabs himself with a bad habit, who opens the arteries of his higher life with the lancet of his passions and drains them of the vital fluid, who inserts his head within the noose of appetite and swings himself off from the pedestal of his self-control, must endure the suffering, the weakness, and the loss which are the issue of his insane conduct.

Now there is nothing which grips one so tightly, nothing which coils itself around one with so deadly a compression, as remorse. When this feeling gets the fingers of its agony upon a man's throat, death itself is a release and a happy deliverance. I do not suppose that any of you can gauge the pressure of this sensation. It is the law of our nature that we cannot realize what we have not felt. Pain is its own interpreter. There is but one oracle through which agony can express its thoughts: that oracle is itself. To know what remorse is, you must have felt remorse. The scarred and blasted tree reveals the hot and withering violence of the lightning, and so the scathed and shattered soul manifests the ruin of sin. I said I did not suppose that any of you could estimate the terrible character of this sensation, for you have never felt it in its extreme bitterness. But many, perhaps all of us, have felt it in part. Recall each of you, then, that period of your life the memory of which is most painful; that lapse, that deed, that connivance with evil, that evasion of duty, that hour of evil pressure and of evil inclination, which most hurt you and others. Bring back and place clearly before you that dire experience. Unbar the gates of your secrecy, and utter to your own mind and heart that long-repressed confession. What humiliation there is in that recollection! What a frightful appearance that lapse has in memory! How it gibbers and shakes its finger at you, as if it had escaped the bondage of its cowardly reticence, and become a part of the world's free and scornful knowledge! I do not sit in judgment on your conduct. I pronounce no verdict. This is not an arraignment, but an illustration. I only ask you to allow the remembrance of that day, that hour, that deed, to assist your imagination to realize what that remorse must be which follows upon greater lapses and darker crimes. I do not wonder that men redden daggers with their own blood, when, looking through the brazen gateway of such a recollection, I behold the lurid fires and glowing pavement which overhang and illuminate with direful light the path beyond. I wonder most at the endurance of the human will, which, with agony here, and no hope in the hereafter, bears up under the pressure of its self-incurred curse. Where can a man with this remorse in his bosom flee? Can he escape his own heart? Can he triumph over his own thought? Can he sweep away the impending terror of his own forebodings? If he should take the wings of the morning, and fly to the uttermost parts of the earth, what would that avail? If he should mount into heaven, if he should swoop to the nethermost recess of hell, neither the light of the firmament, nor the depth of the bottomless pit itself, could provide him refuge from the terror of his own consciousness. My hearers, a man with this remorse of sin in his heart is the movable centre of a contracting circumference. The fire of his torment girdles him about, and over its blazing border he can never leap. Wherever he moves, it moves with him. The evil which kindled feeds it, and the fire of his suffering will never be quenched. Now, who can deliver him from his punishment? Can you or I? Is there a man or woman here equal to this task? It may be a brother, but can you feel that brother's remorse? It may be a loved one: can you bear the agony of her self-conviction? No. That soul stands alone, like an oak on the plain when the bolt hangs suspended and about to be launched above it. The fire will come down, and every leaf shall be withered. The very trunk shall be rived, and upon it shall fall the concentrated violence of the storm. So upon that soul shall the judgment of Heaven descend, and it must bear the burden of the Almighty's wrath. The lesson I wish to teach, is the individual responsibility of your acts before God. In morals there is no copartnership, no *pro rata* division of profit and loss. Each man receives according to the summation of his own account. By as much as any of you have done wrong, for that wrong you yourself are responsible. If you have sown to the wind, upon you alone will fall the pressure of the whirlwind. If your virtue is weak, if your will is irresolute, if your appetites are strong, the battle is your own, and by you must the battle be fought out. If you have wronged anybody, if you have slighted anybody, if you have betrayed anybody, if you have tempted or ruined anybody, — the sin stands ghastly and ominous at your own door. Others may have done as ill, others may have done worse, but their evil or their well doing is no defence for you. Each soul is a unit, and virtue is absolute. The oak cannot borrow a leaf from the maple, the fruitful cannot lend to a barren tree. The solemnity of this thought is beyond expression. When our souls shall stand naked before God, the heavens will concentrate upon us their attention. Every heart that is condemned shall be condemned by itself. The sins that we have nursed will give their testimony against us, and wickedness will acquiesce in the justice of its own condemnation. In view of that final arbitrament, I ask you all to look within your own hearts, and ascertain definitely what your condition is. Learn to-night what breezes waft your ship, what pilot holds the helm, and whither you are bound.

Enlist imagination in this service. Separate yourself from all your kind, make of the world a solitude, depopulate the globe, and think of yourself as the only living soul upon which the attention of Heaven and Hell is fixed to-night. With all these innumerable eyes fastened upon you, bearing the inquisition of the universe, with the scrutiny of the All-seeing Himself directed like a single beam of light upon your soul, tell me, what is your condition and your hope? Are you prepared for the hereafter? If to-night its massive gates should open, and the dark-faced usher summon you to appear, could you pass beneath its gloomy portal fearlessly and at peace? Are you ready to go, sin-covered as you are, and take your stand before the great white throne? Would your heart fail and your limbs falter in that hour of supreme emergency? Here and now I say to you, wishing to suggest no fear to supply you with a motive to act, that, if this subject has not been canvassed, — if this great problem, — the greatest that ever engaged human thought, the problem which includes all other problems in it as the whole includes the parts, — if this has not been solved, you are living neither in accordance with the injunction of revelation nor the dictates of common prudence. That man or woman,

I care not of what faith, of what profession, of what mode of thought, who does not take the last element of risk out of the future, acts against the promptings of ordinary caution. The man who does not analyze the possibilities of the future down to the last drop, in order to extract therefrom some well-ascertained hope, is a marvel of lethargy and indiscretion. As beings able to think, challenged to thought by as supreme a motive as ever quickened intellect, I exhort you to sink the plummet of your investigation into the depth of this question to-night. Touch bottom somewhere. Reach some kind of a conclusion; and let this stand as a white day in the calendar of your time, because, between the rising and going down of the sun thereof, you ascertained, for the first time in your life, your moral condition, and fixed by an unalterable decision the character of your future destiny.

I have alluded to the individuality of moral responsibility. I have striven to show you that each one must endure his own sufferings, and abide the result of his own actions, and that in this no one can share with him. Not only is this true in respect to moral responsibility, but it is equally true in respect to moral growth.

You may place two trees side by side, so that their branches shall interlace, and the fragrance of their blossoms intermingle, and yet in their growth each is separate. Covered by the same soil, moistened by the same drop, warmed by the same ray, the roots of either collect and reinforce the trunks of each, with their respective nourishment. Each tree grows by a law of its own growth, and the law of its own effort. The sap of one in its upward or downward flow cannot desert its own channels and feed the fibres of the other. So it is with two Christians. Planted in the same soil, drawing their sustenance from the same source, they, nevertheless, extract it through individual processes of thought and life. In daily contact and communion, whether in floral or fruitful states intermingling, equal in girth and height, equal in the results of their growth, the spiritualized currents of the one mind cannot become the property of the other. They cannot exchange duties. They cannot exchange hopes. They cannot exchange rewards, and, when lifted by Divine transplanting into another soil and clime, the law which governed, which divided, which individualized them here, will govern, divide, and individualize them there. No matter how close may be the communion between my soul and other souls; no matter how intimate and sympathetic may be my relation to you and yours, to me, still it remains true that whatever growth I have is my own growth; the hope which cheers me, is my own hope; the reward which awaits me, if reward shall be mine, will be eternally my own reward. It is also true that in struggle, in peril, in temptation, in battle, assist as you may, petition as you may, exhort as you may, the ultimate act, the critical decision, is of my own will.

Against the future, represented by your weakness and indwelling sin, set your face, then, O Christian, with a grim and intensely personal sentiment of determination. Cover yourself with your own self-sustained and self-advanced shield. When set upon by anything hostile, seek the shelter of no one's back, but look steadfastly into the eyes and strike boldly out at the person of your foe. I find nothing in Scripture which warrants me to seek alliance with others, in order to escape the necessity of utmost personal endeavor. Seeking only to know that you are covered with the whole armor of God, go into battle single-handed and alone. Whatever cup God commends to your lips, whether bitter or sweet, drink it, looking to no one for encouragement. Draw your inspiration from your own convictions of duty. Live self-collected; live within yourself. Then, when the roar of the battle dies out in your ears, and your spirit stands poised expectant, ready to mount above the tumult forever, you will be able to say, leaving it to swell the mighty memories of moral triumph, "I have fought the good fight, I have finished the course."

This does not seem to be the prevailing view of Christians living in the churches to-day. Undue importance, as it appears to me, is attached to the connection of Christians one with another, and to the good or bad effect such connection has upon individual growth. Men seek and depend upon alliance with others, as if in that alliance they could find security from evil, and support other than that which comes through personal watchfulness and effort. They act as if a failure to receive such assistance as they deem proper released them from obligation, or at least furnished a palliation of their own failure. Young or weakly Christians are apt to fall into this error. They are prone to attribute their slow development or non-development to the lethargy of the church, or to their failure to receive such cordial assistance as the covenant suggests and they have reason to expect. I do not say that there is not a certain modicum of truth in this complaint, which, in one way or another, so often comes to a pastor's ears. It is undoubtedly true, that the covenant is not lived up to in this respect. Multitudes who connect themselves with the churches do not receive that fellowship and love which our covenants and the professed object of church organization lead one to anticipate; and it behooves us to give due heed to this complaint, and so act as to make it impossible. But when you have granted the utmost that one can rightfully claim in this respect, when you have acknowledged all that you justly can concerning it, still you will find that the complaint is often based upon a misapprehension of spiritual relations and the causes of spiritual growth. This cannot be too deeply impressed on a convert's mind, that in his own natural powers, directed and sanctified by the Spirit, he is to find the source of all his usefulness, his safety, and his growth. Those processes of thought through which the Christian's mind passes upward in understanding of God and apprehension of duty are strictly and absolutely individual. I cannot think for you, or you for me. We cannot ponder, we cannot meditate, for one another. Soul food, like body food, is assimilated by each man for himself. You might as well insist that I could feed you by what I take into my own system, as that the pabulum which my mental activity secures for my own growth can minister to you nourishment. Material wealth can be transferred, property can be willed to you, and you can be enriched by the result of another's toil; but no one can transfer his thought-power to another. You cannot transmit mental capacity on parchment. You cannot reward idleness with the fruit of consecrated endeavor. In all these respects religion is intensely personal. Whether you rear a hovel or a palace, it must stand on foundations your own hands have hewn and laid, and the mortar which cements the structure must be moistened by the sweat of your own industry. I wish every young Christian here to-night, yea, and every old one too, would bring this truth home upon his consciousness, that in this respect he cannot divide responsibility with another. His church may be lethargic, his pastor may be remiss, he may receive rebuff where he expected sympathy, and fellowship be only in name, and yet he is held to the same accountability, he must be judged by the same standard of duty and growth. Our graces may be as lifeless as the leaves of a blasted tree, and yet he is to be perpetually green. We may fall together, or one by one; yet over the ruins of our prostrated hopes the turrets of his citadel are to rise.

The great end of all teaching to-day should be to make the membership of our churches individually strong. In the realization of that result lies the hope of the future. The generations to come are to be generations subject to great temptations. Like an orchard of young trees planted on the northern slope of a mountain, our children will grow up in a morally hazardous exposure. A nation of cities, where masses of men are crowded together, — where wealth begets injurious luxury, and poverty leads to crime, — where travel is a popular custom and a popular necessity, — where nothing is permanent, nothing is settled, — is a country where virtue must be strictly individual, if it is to survive at all. We must remember that much which contributed to the assistance of morality in our fathers' day is no longer with us. The home influence, for instance, — the most potent and beneficent sentiment, — will never again be felt as we have felt it. Cities, railroads, and emigration make home impossible. Your children will not derive their gravity, virtues, and health from such sources as were open to you. Between the young man of 1840 and 1870 is a vast gulf of change, — let us hope, of progress. The tide ahead runs with whirling swiftness, and the air is full of drifting spray and patches of froth. Those who sail the future must beat their way up in the teeth of the tempest. Men and women that stand erect under such pressure as awaits the next generation will stand because of some other reason than that they are church-members, or because they are restrained by the fear of public opinion. God alone knows what public opinion will be forty years from this. Such as stand will stand because they are strong in themselves. They will stand, as the granite pillar stands, because it is weighty and ponderous, and set upon a well-secured pedestal. I have no faith in a virtue strong only in crutches and props, which topples over the instant friendly outside support is withdrawn. The soul that is virtuous only becaue of the absence of temptation is not virtuous at all; but the soul that looks enticement steadily in the eye, and frowns it down, until it slinks away abashed, which has the offer but refuses the bribe, — to that soul the struggle and the triumph is divinely strong. His virtue is not an accident. It is the result of that heroic self-control which follows the impartment of the Spirit.

Who of you here to-night are thus strong? Whose piety is of that broad-chested sort which has sufficient lung-room for the healthy inspiration of the whole system? Whose practice in spiritual gymnastics is so well sustained as to keep every joint supple, every tendon flexile, and every artery in healthy beat? Nothing stirs the spirit of admiration and reverence in me more than to see a young man of twenty lower himself down to the weights, clasp the handles, and lift six hundred pounds. How the creative skill and benevolence of God are brought out by such an exhibition of physical power! When you see a little man of one-hundred-and-fifty-pound weight elevate a mass of iron and lead, every bone perpendicularly adjusted in its socket, every muscle ridging out, every little vein flushing with rose-tints the clear, transparent skin, you realize the statement of Holy Writ, that man is wonderfully and fearfully made.

But, friends, there is a soul-power more wonderful, more majestic, more divine, than all physical power. There is a nobler sight than a well-tended, well-developed body. It is the spectacle of a well-tended, well-developed spirit. And there is no exhibition so beautiful or so magnetic in its influence under heaven, as that which a soul presents when it lowers itself to the weight of some adversity, some dead, inert mass of selfishness, and lifts it; and, with a pressure on it sufficient to crush a weakly one, and cause it to cry out in pain, stands erect, evenly poised, firmly planted, Godlike. I know some men and women who have lived in the grip of a vice-like pressure for twenty years, and not a sound has escaped their lips, not a look revealed to any the burden they were staggering under. I know men unto whom temptation to cheat and lie, and put a price in money or sensual pleasure upon their virtue, has come up in confidence, and, like a braggart, challenged them to the test; and they have accepted the challenge, and without running behind some other man's back, or the back of the church, or any other protection, have stripped for a fair fight, and locked in with it; and, assisted of God, who never deserted a man yet with such a spirit in him, have thrown it and dashed the life out of it. Such Christians never have to fight many battles. Like Christ Himself, they have their hour in the portico of the Temple, and their struggle on the mountain's crest, and perchance a night of agony in some Gethsemane; but their life, on the whole, is calm, and confident, and full of surpassing peace.

Now I hold such a self-reliant spirit up to-night as an example for you, — especially for you who are young, and you, too, who are weak and tempted. Here is where the heroism of Christian living comes in. Here is where the triumph and the victory appear. That man who cannot control his passions when in full career, who cannot curb his temper and rein in his appetites, who cannot send the cloud back into the heavens and scatter it in golden mist, has never felt the first thrill of kingship.

I wish you all to feel — I wish to feel myself — our personal responsibility in this matter. If any of you have been doing wrong, you must break off, and break off, too, by an act of your own will. Upon you God puts to-night the burden of decision. I may sympathize, I may warn, I may entreat, but I cannot decide for you. O that I could! How quickly, then, would I heave you, by a noble resolution, up to the level of your duty! How quickly would I lift you from the maze of doubt and longing and hesitation, and plant your feet on the firm ground of consecrated endeavor! But, alas! I cannot. I see you beating about in the fog, and I can only stand afar off, on the shore, at the mouth of the harbor, and shout to you the direction: "Ho, men and women! Ho, brothers; this way, this way! Steer for the light that streams from the Cross!" Ah me! ah me! the winds and waves beat back my voice, and you, all heedless of peril, are being buffeted and driven hither and thither while the precious moments are passing.

See what determination the world manifests in pursuit of carnal things; over what sharp obstacles men mount to honor and wealth. A worldly man asks no help from another. He plays the game of life boldly, asking no odds. When he comes to an obstruction, he puts his shoulder bravely against it, and rolls it aside or climbs over it. Nay, more, out of the very fragments of previous overthrow he erects a triumph. Nothing overawes him nor discourages him. He asks no one to bear his burden. He bears it himself, and finds it to be a source of strength and power. And shall a Christian shrink from what a worldling bravely attempts? Shall we unto whom the heavens minister faint, when those to whom the gates of power are shut persevere? My brethren, these things ought not so to be. What is a slip? What is a scar? What is a fall? They will all testify to the perils you endured and the heroism of your perseverance, at the Last Day. Think not of these. Write on your banner, where, living or dying, your eyes shall behold them, these words: "He who endureth unto the end *shall be saved*."

But, friends, who made it possible for us to bear our burdens? Who taught us by the wisdom of His lips? Who, by the example of His life and death? It was Jesus. He bore His burden when He cried in the Garden, "If it be possible, let this cup pass from Me." No, neither the sympathy of Heaven nor the power of God delivered Him. He accepted the destiny of His condition; He set His lips to the bitter cup, and drained it to the very dregs. But how came He, the Innocent One, the Holy One, to have any burden? Had He committed sin that He must groan under the judgment? No; His nature was as white as a lily when it floats on a darkened tide. The Law of God had no claim against Him. He had not trangressed, He had not violated, the least injunction of the Almighty. He had wronged no one; He had slighted no one; He had neglected no one. How came He, then, to have a burden? and whose burden was it that He bore? My hearer, it was your burden and mine that He bore. Heaven had claims against us, and He out of love and compassion undertook to satisfy those claims. He did satisfy them. It was decreed that He must leave Heaven for a time, and He left it. It was decreed that He must take the lot and condition of a mortal, and He took them. It was decreed that He must die, and the blood of His most precious life was freely shed on Calvary. All this was done for us. I mean every one of you,—for you who accept and for you who reject Him. He was the only man who ever died for his enemies. And now, with all that Christ did for you to point and wing it, I launch this query straight home to your hearts, What have you done for Him? Have you loved Him? Have you served Him? Have you ever even gone and done so much as to express a word of gratitude to Him? Do you feel any gratitude? Why, a dog is thankful for the bread you give him, and, faithful unto death to his benefactor, he will lie down in the mountains by your side and die. And yet there are some of you unto whom that dog might well be taken as a teacher and an example. The wind will soon come up from the south balmy and warm, bearing in its breath suggestions of the orange and the rose, and every root and fibre will thrill in welcome, and the dry twigs swell and prepare to unfurl their green banners, and the buds, unable to restrain themselves longer, will burst into beauty and fragrance. Shall Nature thus hasten to express her gratitude to God as the sun comes journeying up from the tropics, and shall we, over whom that love is ever at its meridian, raying down its invitation upon us, quickening us with sweet enticements of growth, remain silent, unmoved, and thankless? O that this coming week might prove a spiritual spring-time to your souls! May we be quickened in our graces, and all the dead things in us start into new life, and our hearts, warmed into energy, know a great blossoming of hope and holy impulse, — fore-runners of great spiritual fruitage!

But, before I close, a word of cheer, a word of hope and consolation.

My friends, it is true I know little of your lives, little of your trials, little of the burdens under which with varying strength you have walked thus far. But life has a stern discipline for all, and as I look into your faces, you seem to me as if each of you was carrying some weight. What struggle, I say to myself, what effort, what manifold phases of experience, what sighs and groans and agonies unexpressed, such a vast audience as this must represent! What lines of recollection, radiating from this hall, run backward to other days and scenes! What memories, starting from the past, throng in upon us here, and hover like a vast cloud of invisible witnesses over us, until every man beholds the record of his life, written as at the Judgment, in living light above his head. And I think of that future which awaits us, of the days yet to be ours, moving in silent and measured procession out of eternity, and of that day of days, which shall be the last, and close the calendar of our toil forever. Live so as to think of that day with joy. It is not for me to speculate as to what death will bring us. I imagine that it will bring us far more than most of us think. At least this much we know, it will bring to the weary and the heavy-laden rest, and to such as missed the fulfilment here a renewal of all their hopes. You will meet with those who journeyed on, being called first, before you, — the brave, the gentle, and the good; and all that to-night is sweet in hope or dear in expectation, if it be pure and cherished purely, will come and put its arms around you, and you will have it with you as yours eternally. And unto all this and much beside, yea, unto this vast temple of life and love, with its magnificent entablatures and majestic spaces, you who enter will enter through one door, Christ Jesus, our Lord and our Redeemer. For unto the city, in which it is builded, with its many gates, each gate a solid pearl, none can climb by any other way. For He is the Way, the Truth, and the Life.

SERMON VI.

NEARNESS OF GOD.

"Thou art near, O Lord." — PSALM cxix. 151.

THE basis of this declaration is the greatness and goodness of God. It is an ejaculation founded on the conviction that in God exist such powers of observation and such faculties that nothing escapes his notice, nothing is beyond his control.

Nature accepts this declaration of faith. She willingly testifies to the presence of a First Cause. In her every form and order of life you find the suggestion of Creative Power. Matter is dead, inert. In it of itself is no faculty of action. It must be acted upon, it must be vitalized, before the spirit of combination, the impulse of life, enters into it. To this formula, this creed, every living substance assents.

The human mind receives the same idea readily. The imagination uses this conception in many lovely and reverential ways. The very senses of the body rejoice at the thought, and are spiritualized by it. In the operation of laws all around us, which could not of themselves have sprung into existence, and the ceaseless energy of which must have been derived from some outside propulsion, the mind recognizes the omnipresence of the Creator. Inanimate substances in their dumb processes of growth and change confess to the same sentiment. The tree says, God is near me, for I am by nature senseless and powerless. I am but so much dead matter operated upon by forces uncaused by and unknown to me. In my substance, in root, trunk, or bough, is no power to occasion such a change as is coming over me. See, it says, — and every leaf and twig speaks, — see the transformation going on among my branches! Behold the addition every hour makes to my appearance! And thus the tree rejoices in God's nearness, and all nature re-echoes the same devout sentiment.

It is of this Divine nearness to man I would speak to-night. It is not my purpose to construct an argument or make a labored analysis. It is not logical demonstration so much as suggestion that I have in view this evening. A sermon is not a boat which an audience can get into and sail off securely on a pleasant intellectual voyage of an hour. It is food to satisfy soul-hunger, to strengthen present weakness, to revive faintness, to soothe pain as it is now felt, and illuminate gathering darkness. At least I would that this should prove so.

My hope is to make some of you realize more

fully than you do now that God is near you, and near you in love, and will be all the days of your coming life.

I would suggest, in the first place, that God is near us in the hour of human desertion.

The Psalms of David are wonderful in the manifold expression they give to human feeling on the one hand, and the Divine nature on the other. Some of them are to God what lakes are to the surrounding and overhanging mountains,— a mirror in which we behold Him reflected. There is one passage found in the twenty-seventh Psalm, by which I have been more comforted, and in which I have seen a more lovely reflection of God, than in any one passage of the whole Bible. I refer to the verse where the writer is speaking of his faith in God's love. He says: "When my father and my mother forsake me, then the Lord will take me up." What a picture of God that is! When my mother forsakes me! How the mind pauses and shrinks at the suggestion! My mother forsake me, I say to myself, mother forsake me! Never! What! that mother who gave me birth, rejoicing in the pain which ushered me to life, who gave of her life to strengthen mine, and woke my infant mind to thought, who bore with all my wild, now often-repented disobedience, who toiled and watched for me, — that mother who sits far off to-night with her Bible on her knees perhaps, her wrinkled and shrivelled hands resting on it, her head streaked with silvery hair, and her lips moving both in thanksgiving and prayer for me now, — mother forsake me! Never! But, my friends, if it were possible; if the sweet current of her endless love could flow back upon itself, and leave me panting upon the sand; if some great sin, some heavy and swift-smiting crime, smote me down and left me bruised and bleeding; and father should come, and, seeing me, curse one who had dishonored his name, and pass by; and mother, pausing only a moment to wring her hands and groan, pass on too; — then the Lord, yea, God who sits in the heavens, who hates sin but loves the sinner infinitely, — God, coming after father and mother, would stoop and take me up. Yet this is the God that some of you will not love, some of you will not serve; yea, this is the God of the Orthodox churches, whom some of you say we make a hard, unfeeling tyrant, rejoicing in the punishment of men.

Human desertion and loneliness of spirit, — who at one time or another has not passed through such seasons? who has not shivered under its cloud, and come dripping and chilled out of the waters of its despair? Even Christ was deserted, and bore the agony of the Garden and trial unassisted by friends. Loneliness is often the result of our own states and moods or circumstances. The mind makes its own solitude, its own despair, and repels human approach. Who admits the world to the secrecy of his thoughts? Who permits the crowd to rush against and force the fastenings of his soul's reticence, and hear its whispered doubts and fears, its terrors and its self-accusations? No one. The fool babbles, but the mouth of the capable is shut. Half our lives the world knows nothing of, and would not understand if they did know. Now and then one like unto ourselves is admitted into the circle of our inner life, and carries about with him the knowledge of our experience; but it lies down and sleeps in the grave when he sleeps. Our very position, by the force of nature or circumstance, is often repellant, and the scorn or sympathy of the world is turned back, as the rain which beats or the warm air which floats up against the sides of the house is turned back therefrom when the windows are closed. We have protection from the rain, it is true, but we lose the fragrance of the perfume.

But there are times when this isolation is made more complete because of surrounding circumstances. A great sorrow the source of which we may not tell, a disappointment which we must conceal, a lapse which we must cover up, a knowledge we must hide, or an appetite which we must combat, but whose presence we must not declare, — each or all of these can produce the same result. Many of you, perhaps, understand the philosophy of this statement. You recognize the accuracy of the analysis. You have stood the centre of some black circle, and felt the agony of the all-surrounding pressure, and you know how powerless the world is to help you at such moments; how all the wires along which the currents of sympathy ordinarily flow are cut or made useless by the raging of the storm, so that human affection can send no message of love, no word of guidance or cheer, — the mother is powerless to help the child, the wife the husband, or the husband the wife. At the two extremes, at the height and depth of human feeling, the soul stands alone. When lifted upon the crest of some great emotion, or when sunk in the depth of despair, its isolation is complete, it is too far above or below the ordinary level of life to hear or heed its voice.

It seems to be God's will that at the supreme moments of our lives we should be alone with Him. Moses must die unattended, and the Christ must bear the agony of the Garden when His disciples were heavy with sleep. The great decisions of our lives are made when alone, and their great griefs are borne with our heads buried in the pillow. More than once are we exiled from the world. More than once have we less than an island for our home, and a loneliness more deep, more oppressive, than the absence of human faces, and the limitless reach of water, weighs us down.

But, friends, we are never in reality alone, never in reality deserted. On our right hand and on our left the Invisible walks. When we stand on the summit of our highest joy, the Ineffable is with us; and when we lie in the depth and darkness of our despair, the Divine Radiance is there. To the wicked this thought is a terror, but to the good and those who would be good it is a joy and consolation. The fool hath said in his heart, "There is no God!" and he repeats it, hoping by repetition to believe the lie; but he never believes it, and he knows it is a lie. Like a snake in torture, he kills himself by the poison of his own fangs. But the good and those who would be good say each with a gladness no voice can ever express, "The Lord is my shepherd; I shall not want." The soul of the Christian, confirmed in its faith, and strengthened by the grace of God, breaks into song in dying, and, like a swan, whose closing note is the sweetest, exclaims, "Thy rod and Thy staff they comfort me!" O the joy of His nearness! O the glory of His presence, in the light of which darkness melts, and that gloom which men so dread brightens into radiance as they pass away!

I remark, in the second place, that God is near to us in the hour of temptation.

The existence and operation of a divine influence is no more surely taught in the Scripture than is the presence of an evil influence. The angelic and demoniacal influence appear side by side along the whole course of Scripture narrative, as two clouds appear at times in the heavens, — the one charged with positive, the other with negative electricity, and darting into each other's bosom, as they move along, their fiery opposition. From Eden to Christ, from Genesis to Revelation, the same antagonism of spiritual forces is seen; and to-day we are subject to the same hostile forces. Experience demonstrates this. How often we have stood conscious of this pressure from either side! How frequently we have felt that influences opposite in tendency and character were bringing each its distinct action to bear upon us, and our wills and feelings were swayed as ships anchored where two converging currents meet! For days, perhaps for weeks, we have thus stood, our decision held at equal poise by opposite motives, or oscillating up and down as the higher or lower preponderated.

No one who has ever debated a question of duty, seeking how to avoid it, no one who has ever had a temptation of any sort, can doubt that in the moral world are two opposite forces, ever at work, and at work, too, on him. Even Jesus was not exempt from this. The established order of things was not modified even to accommodate Him. He was tempted in all points like as we are, yet without sin.

Now no one can order the time and character

of his temptations. An oak might as well try to order the force and direction of the gale that shall next bear down on it, as for any one of you to attempt to say what shall be the nature and strength of that temptation which to-morrow shall entice us. That is one of the chief sources of our weakness. Now and then, it is true, a great cloud rolls up from a fixed point, and we know which way to scud and what sails to take in. But not unfrequently the blackness is spread over the entire heavens, and not a flash or single jar warns us from what quarter the danger is to come. And there is not a person here to-night who can tell whether he will be tempted on this or that side of his nature to-morrow, or whether the pressure will be too strong for him or not.

Now there is, as I judge, a very prevalent feeling that, when a man is being tempted, he is deserted of God. I need not discuss the origin of this view. I will remark only concerning the effect of it on the tempted person himself, and what I regard as the true view.

Now the very feeling that the Tempter wishes to produce in the person's mind at the time of his being tempted is that he is deserted of God. In that thought lies half the force of the temptation. The fallen or falling man is made to feel that the heavens are black toward him, that God hates him on account of his sins, that he has fallen too far ever to recover, and is given over as lost. Well does Satan know that from this thought will spring a kind of wild recklessness, a desperation of mind, a sort of mad *abandon* to sin in its license, which will confirm and harden him in every wicked course and practice.

Now, friends, that is not my theology. I have no idea that the arm of God is around me save when I totter, but that the instant I begin to reel he withdraws it, and leaves me to stand or fall as it may chance. Heaven is no idle spectator of human struggles, and at every crisis of my life invisible hands have girded my loins and strengthened the braces of my shield. When an army goes forth to battle, a true leader goes forth with it; and never did a man go out to do battle for truth and right, who did not hear, as he advanced, the chariot of the Almighty rolling up close behind him. In the supreme moment of his destiny, whether of downfall or triumph, God always stands by a follower. When Satan draws nigh a soul in enmity, God draws nigh in its defence. When evil triumphs, beats down your guard, strikes you to the ground, and stands fiendishly victorious, a shield is ofttimes suddenly thrust between the soul and his uplifted arm, and the foe retires baffled and chagrined. How many such deliverances some of us can recall! How many such escapes we have had!

I do not mean to say that a man may not so abuse and outrage Divine forbearance as to be irrevocably hardened and given over of God. Sin may, undoubtedly, so far produce its logical results, even in this life, as to take the very productive powers of virtue out of the soul. As it is with a barren and sandy plain from which the wind has scooped the nourishing soil, so that not even a tuft of grass relieves the fierce glitter of the noonday sun, so it is possible that here and there a man may be living with not a virtue, or the germ of a virtue, in his soul. But such a being, if such there is, is not a man ; he is a monster. He personifies, not sin, but the result of sin, yea, of sin long indulged and persisted in.

But, my hearers, such do not form the rule ; they are the exceptions. Men are not monsters, earth is not hell, and the full manifestation of the logical and ultimate result of sin upon character is not beheld here. The human soul is like an instrument of music jangled and out of tune. It needs retuning. It needs the master's hand and the master's touch. The strings are not torn from the frame. The keys are not displaced. They are not loosened. The discord comes from their temporary condition. A fall, a jar, a wrench, has wrought confusion. Set them in order, bring them up to the line of the correct note ; then sweep them, and what melody, what power, what liquid sweetness of sound shall come out of them !

Now you let a man fall into this condition, and what does God do ? desert him, leave him, let him alone, give him up ? Why *no,* that is not Heaven's way. Why, think what man has cost God, what He has done for him already. The best gauge of man's value is the effort God has put forth in his behalf. Put Calvary, put all the prophets from Moses down, put all the efforts of the Holy Ghost, in one scale, and man in the other ; and the balance gives the Divine estimate of the human soul, yea, of your soul and mine. Who here thought God loved him that much ? What one dreamed that His determination to save him amounted to that ?

Now when God sees a man or woman struggling with temptation, sees you about to fall, sees the wreck and ruin which will result unless He comes to your rescue, do you think He stands aloof, indifferent and regardless how it shall go with you ? Do you think Christ could have allowed Peter to sink ? Why, the very buoyancy would have gone out of Christ Himself, if He had coolly withheld Himself from His disciple's rescue. There is not an element of the Divine nature, there is not one amid the multitude of His mercies, which does not mean help and support and salvation to you and me, in the hour of our deepest need. There is a lily, — He is thoughtful of that. Yet, what is a lily ? Pluck it ; fling its leaves into the air ; stand and idly watch them as the white fragments of its parted beauty drift down the wind. What has the world lost? The air is not less sweet, the earth is not less fair. There is a bird, — a little bunch of tuneful down. Even in mid flight, in mid song, it rolls upon its back, and falls fluttering to the earth. A drop of blood is on its breast, two ruffled plumes in its broken wing; it gasps once, a convulsion quivers through its little frame, it closes its eyes and dies. You walk on. You forget it. You wake next morning. The garden is as full of song. Your ears miss no note. Yet God saw and noted that little bird go down.

Do you think that He who clothes the lily and sees when it is torn, He who keeps watch over the birds, and sees when each one falls, has no care, no thought, no sympathy for your soul and mine when an evil power comes up to blacken it, and kill it, yea, take all the fragrance and song out of it? No! no! Such a being is not my God. Neither in supplication nor in praise are my hands lifted to such a being. My friend, I dare to say that there are black days ahead of me, that the future will be as the past, and that more than once I shall stand in great peril and near death; but there never will come an hour, from this moment to my dying gasp, whether I live rightly or wrongfully, when God will not stand in love by my side, when all a father can do will not be done to save me from danger, and my soul from death.

Furthermore, the nearness of God to us is seen in the various experiences of our life and growth. Now it is hard to analyze the sources and causes of growth. Ask the rose how it grows. Say to it, "Whence came your sweetness and the royal color of your leaves?" and the rising volume of its fragrance is your only answer. It cannot say how much it owes to the sun, how much to the shower, how much to the cloud, nor whether day or night brought most of perfume and beauty to it. So it is with the soul. You ask one of these aged Christians here, — that sweetest one of us all, that one best tinted and ripened for heaven, — whence came her purity, her patience, her calm reliance and that hope of hers which shines in the horizon of her closing life luminous as the evening star, when it hangs like a great opal on the western rim of the heavens, — and can she tell you? No! Whether God was nearer to her in youth or age, in joy or grief, in hours of obedience or the uprising of great rebellions, in sickness or health, strength or weakness, she knoweth not. She only knows that she is as she is through the grace of God.

This thought is full of the plumage of golden wings, and lifts the heavy-hearted up. You may grope in darkness or walk in light, but He unto whom the light and darkness are one is ever with you. You may moan or rejoice, but that ear, sensitive to every human cry, hears you the same. You may be standing erect, with the flush of a great triumph in your eyes, or lying prone in the dust crushed under a greater defeat; but the Lord is with you still. The heavens may be warm or cold, the air filled with sunshine or driving sleet; you may come like a lamb healthy and white from play, or crawl to the door soiled with dirt and gore, and cruelly torn by wolves, but the Shepherd is ready to admit and welcome you to the fold.

Is there some one in this audience, then, whose nature is torn and stained? Indeed, who of us is white and whole? Is there a man or woman here who has been in the last years of his life like a sheep among wolves, and who is ready to fly from danger and pain to the fold of God's love to-night? If so, I bid you come. Come as I came. Come just as you are. Wait for nothing, but *come.* Do you think that the blood on the fleece, and the marks of the teeth on the throat ever kept a sheep from the fold, ever caused it to be turned away? And do you imagine that the failures of your past, the ghastly secrets of your life, the scars of your sinfulness, the taint of your inward defilement, will cause Christ to turn you away? My friend, never believe it.

Answer me this, Did a mother ever send a child away because it was hungry? Did a father ever disown a boy because he was sick and in pain?

And did God ever refuse to pardon a sinner because he was sinful? What does your heart say? What does the Bible say? Say! It says that God "would not that any should perish; but that all might come to the knowledge of the truth and live."

O the power of that blood shed on Calvary! Who can estimate it? Is there any scarlet so deep that it will not wash it white as snow? Is the crimson of any guilt so red that, touched by it, the crimson shall not be white as wool? Ask the thief how he came to be in heaven, and he will say, "The blood admitted me here." Ask Paul if it was his labor, his self-denial for the truth's sake, his unflinching constancy, or his heroic virtues, which gained him the crown he wears and the fadeless wreath? And he will exclaim, "No, brother, no! it was not my constancy, nor my self-denial, nor my labors and sufferings; the blood alone gained me all this." That was the equivalent which satisfied Divine justice, and gave to mercy the opportunity of exercise. And how will any of us gain that entrance to heaven for which we hope? By our prayers, think you? by our works? by any worth or worthiness in us? I warn you not to believe it. On the merits of the blood, if at all, we shall stand acquitted before God.

But some say that there is no need of the blood.

My friends, does the soiled garment need the soap? does the withered and dying grass need rain? does the earth need the sun? does guilt need pardon? Then do you and I, and every soul that has acted out its nature in sinfulness, need the atoning, reconciling blood of the Saviour. Why, look at your past. I speak to you who have been tossed about on the wild waves of life, who have been lifted and cast down, who have suffered and sinned. So far as the world knows, so far as the world judges, it is an easy, innocent, and comfortable past. But in the light of Heaven, in the light of our consciences, in the light of our own knowledge, it is a grim and ghastly past, — a past we dare not show, we dare not face. Who here would live over his past, do over all his old deeds, think over his old thoughts, go through with all his old experiences? Not one. Prepared or unprepared, you say, fit or unfit, the grave is welcome. One life is enough such as I have lived. I have no heart to repeat it. If there is such a thing as purity, if there is such a thing as holiness, if there is such a place as heaven, — their source, their home, their eternal residence, — then must I find a saviour outside and above myself. This is the conviction of every heart that has intelligently measured itself by the Bible standard. If you would know how near God draws to you to-day, behold that He does it in the blood of His Son, in the privileges of this consecrated hour, in the best impulses of your hearts, in the fears of the past we can never wholly escape, in the hopes of that future toward which in thought we fly, as a bird, tired and heavy-laden, with set wings and a glad cry, swoops down to her nest.

I have spoken to you of the nearness of God as a fact in our daily life, but what makes that nearness of none effect? what hand is it that cuts the golden wires along which God telegraphs his messages of love? what is it in our atmosphere which blurs and distorts his face until it becomes a fearful visage to our eyes and full of dread? It is sin; not sin in the abstract, as a principle, but sin as committed, sin as indulged. No man hates you so much, no man shrinks from looking you in the eye so much, as he who has ill treated you. Let a man hate you whom you have injured, and there is an end to his enmity. Reparation frank and full puts an end to his hard feeling toward you, and relays the foundation of prostrated friendship. But let a man hate you without cause, save such as his envy, or spite, or bigotry, or vanity supplies, and his hate is endless. The worst enemy you can have is the man who should be your best friend; that man's enmity is devilish. Between that person and you is a great gulf which his own conduct and feeling have digged; and no generosity, no frankness, no honorable treatment, on your part can bridge it. Well, so it is with us in our wickedness toward God. Sin separates us from Him; sin converts all His love into a source of terror; sin makes the thought of His nearness a dread. By so much as you do wickedly, by so much does God become a being to flee from and avoid; sin takes all the courage out of a man and makes him cowardly. How many have died in agony from this cause! Ay, men robust and brawny, who could look along the glistening barrel into their antagonist's eyes at twelve paces and not flinch, have cried out and screamed, and made the chambers they died in ring with their screams and terror. Why? Why did they shrink from the approaching darkness? Why did their boasting depart and their hearts sink within them as they saw God, whom they had disobeyed and scoffed at and defied, drawing near to them?—why? Because they *had* disobeyed and scoffed at and defied Him. That is why they were frightened and dreaded to enter His presence. That is the whole philosophy of it. If any of you desire to die easily, live rightly, as the Spirit directs; do this, and you will go to your grave as a man weary with honest toil goes to his couch at night, glad that the day at last is ended, and the time for sleep and pleasant dreams has come.

Sin not only separates us from God, but from our fellow-men also. There is something delightful in human fellowship. It is sweet for heart to commune with kindred heart. It is sweet to share our joys and divide our sorrows with those we love; sweet is it to feel that you are known and know; sweet the interchange of thought and sympathy, the mingling of common hopes, the division of burdens and cares. But sin shuts the mouth and closes the heart. It breaks the circuit and interrupts the current. Guilt makes us dumb. Our words by day, our dreams by night, become so many avenues of terror. It divides love from love, and thereby chokes up the very springs of comfort and help. Sin is loneliness. Sin is seclusion. Even fellowship in guilt loosens not the gag. He who goes over Niagara cannot take his friends with him.

Am I correct in this? Is this mere word-painting, or accurate analysis? Frightfully accurate! But, friends, we cannot always conceal our guiltiness; we cannot forever keep our dungeon. The jealously guarded key will at last be snatched from our hand, the doors of our secrecy burst open, and all the hidden things will come trooping out and stand revealed to God and man. What will that shame, what will that exposure be! Mark you, I am not appealing to fear. I seek to spring no trap of conviction upon you. This is statement, not exhortation. This is intellectual analysis,— an attempt to get at the core of the matter, to catalogue and set in array before you the elements and material for future reflection. This is all. Still it is wise to anticipate the future, and, my friend, when the hour of exposure shall come, as it surely will, how will you stand? When all that is in your character shall be revealed, all that you have covered with evasion be dragged forth, all you have veiled be brought under the focus of that last unavoidable investigation, what will be the result? My hearer, you and I may differ on other things, but we, knowing ourselves, know this,— that if you and I are not covered, are not protected in that hour by the mercy of God, we shall stand utterly hopeless,— universally abhorred, and universally condemned. That is our only hope. Should that fail us— I check myself; I have no heart to describe that awful contingency. Some steadier hand than mine must draw the dark perspective which stretches with ever-thickening blackness into eternity.

Here, then, I pause. Into the life which awaits you on the morrow,— if morrow shall be to us,— I dismiss you. Its loneliness, its temptations, its trials, await you at the door. Amid whatever of solitude, amid temptations numberless, amid trials not a few, remember that God is near you. The stars are distant, but God is this side the stars. The heavens are remote, but He who rules them from centre to their outermost circumference walks on your right hand and on your left. Sleeping or waking, laughing or weeping, coming in or going out, the Lord is ever with you. This never forget. On some future day, even that which shall know no night, with a vaster multitude, within a larger temple, by the mercy of God, we may perchance be permitted to meet. Until which time, living ever in hope born of His love, I pray peace be with you, even that peace which the wicked cannot understand, and which passeth not away. Amen.

SERMON VII.

DIVINE FRIENDSHIP.

"A friend of publicans and sinners." — LUKE vii. 34.

THERE are many pleasant relations which men sustain to each other in this world. Human lives meet and mingle, and are interwoven like threads in a texture of glossy richness and manifold colors, and never does human nature appear to better advantage than when seen in the light of its relations and connections. No one thread, no matter of what richness of color, can rival the magnificence of the entire robe.

There, for instance, is the relation between parent and child, and it is regarded the world over with respect and reverence. There, too, is the relation of husband and wife, and when represented by harmony of taste and temperament between the two, you might not find a lovelier exhibition. The relations which exist between brothers and sisters, between the government and the citizen, between the church and its members, — all these are pleasant to contemplate, and are productive of happiness and profit to man.

But there is one other relation man can sustain

to man, which, as a spontaneous and self-created impulse of one soul for another soul, as an evidence of mutual likes and aspirations, and as a proof, in its higher exhibitions of itself, of constancy and unselfish benevolence, is inferior to no other. I refer to the relation which exists between all true friends,— honest, sincere friendship.

In the relation of parent and child, authority on the one hand and obedience on the other occupy the foreground. In man's relation to the government, material interests may preponderate. Love is by nature selfish in its appropriation of its object, — flowing with a swifter and rougher tide. But in friendship, neither authority nor obedience, neither material considerations nor feverish excitement, enter as an inciting cause or result. It flows from source to termination with a deep, even, and ever-widening current, — a safe, a lovely, and a fruitful stream. No wrecks line its shores ; no waves of passion beat mercilessly upon its beach ; no corses float along its current. Society owes to its humanizing influence more than it can ever express, and God regards it with pleasure and complacency.

Now this is the relation which Christ is said to sustain to mankind in our text. In the Bible he is presented to us in many aspects, — as a Judge, a Saviour, a Councillor ; as a Brother, Prophet, Priest and King, — but in this passage he stands forth in the light and garb of a Friend.

Christ as the Friend of man is, therefore, the theme of this discourse.

I do not intend to analyze friendship, and enumerate its elements. I will only suggest one or two of the more prominent. The first of which is Constancy.

A true friend is constant. Circumstances may change and many desert, but he remains the same. You yourself may change. Sickness may sap your powers, misfortune make you its sport, and reduce you to despair. You may be corroded with the rust of the world, but no lapse on your part can divert his sympathy. Let but a cry escape your lips, and he will be at your side. Let a blow be aimed at you, and his will be the hand to throw it up. When other voices clamor to your discredit, his will stem the torrent of abuse, and throw the weight of his reputation and advocacy into the scale of your defence.

Now all this and much more can be said of Christ in His feelings toward every one of you here to-night. I say every one. I do not wish you to understand that Christ is a friend to the good and pure alone, if such there be here; nor to those who are correct in their deportment,—whose virtue walks into men's acknowledgment unquestioned. No; I launch the friendship of Christ out among you to-night as men launch a life-boat among a struggling mass of drowning men, and there is not a hand beating the briny water, swarth or white, that may not seize it, and there is not a sinking soul in this audience that may not appropriate the friendship of the Lord.

Now I suppose some of you have failed. Indeed, we have all failed! But I suppose that some of us have failed more than others. We have been tempted by others, and we have tempted ourselves. We have been pierced by arrows shot at us from a distance, and we have taken knives and opened our own veins. We have fought enemies without, and we have had a greater enemy within, and more than once have we been tempted to say: "It is of no use for me to try to be good. The more I try, the more I fail. I have forfeited my self-respect and God's love long ago. I will give it up."

My friend and brother, don't you give it up. While the Friend of publicans and sinners sits on the judgment-seat, you have no right to despair. Do not be discouraged. His friendship for you is the same — as fresh, as sincere, as strong — to-night as it ever was. Your despondency is cowardly and wicked, and from the Devil. There is not another arrow in his full quiver with which the Adversary pierces so many souls to their death as despair. When a man desponds of being better, when a woman feels that the path to the throne is so steep that she never can climb it, then, if funeral-bells were ever tolled in heaven, might they swing their heaviest dirge. Such despair is utterly groundless, and the Tempter, even as he urges it home upon you, knows it. Doubt father and mother, doubt husband and wife, but never doubt the friendship of the Lord Jesus Christ for your soul. In the still watches of the night, when memory, remorsefully busy, will not let you sleep, out of the darkness shape a celestial figure, and say to it, "Lord, remember me when Thou comest in Thy kingdom"; and in response, breaking the dreadful silence and the spell of your despair, shall sound the words, "Lo, I am with you alway even unto the end of the world."

When your soul wanders in darkness, which its own evil thoughts and deeds have spread over it; when you revolt at confession, and imprison yourself in your own secrecy, go and tell Him of all your struggles and agonies, your failures and crimes, and thus roll the burden off at the foot of the cross. Why at the foot of the cross? Because there it was that His blood fell, — the blood which came from His hands and head and feet, and gushed from His spear-riven side, when He in His own person bore the penalty of human sin, and made atonement to the transgressed law, — the blood which cleanseth whiter than fuller's soap, and, washed in which, your sins and mine, though they be as crimson, shall become as wool.

This constancy and impartiality of Christ's friendship are what make Jesus such a Saviour as He is. This is what makes Him, the world over, and in all ages, so near and dear to His followers; and this, too, it is, which lifts the Gospel plan of the atonement above all philosophies and codes of ethics.

If He was a friend only to the good, or to us only in so far as we are good, what sort of a Saviour would He be? What application would the Gospels have to the race as a race? Philosophy does very well to amuse, and perchance profit the learned. Ethics supply the virtuous with needed and salutary rules of life. But what will you do with those who are neither good nor learned? What would the religion of Horticultural Hall do for the low and vicious, — for the ignorant by reason of neglect, and for the ignorant by reason of circumstance, — for the heathen, and those of us who feel that, if God is just and decides on the merits of a case, we stand guilty and condemned before Him to-night? Is there not a craving, my hearer, in your heart and mine, for a personal Saviour, a living, breathing, ever-constant friend; beside whom rules, maxims, and speculations are no more than dry and scentless rose-leaves are to our nostrils.

Now every life has its different moods and ranges of thought and phases of experience. We do not live on one dead level from cradle to grave; no, nor on the same level any one day through. It is marvellous what sharp changes, what sudden fluctuations, there may be in our experiences between the morning and evening of the same day. I have often thought that, in the character and changes of his life, man is as the sky, now all aflame with the uprising glory of some sun-like impulse, and anon black with clouds and full of tempestuous violence. And what we need is a Saviour who will be a Saviour to us at all times, and in every mood and temper. The friendship we need is a friendship which will be the same in its helpful and saving relations to us, whether we kneel at the altar or stand white and haggard on the scaffold's edge.

This brings us to the second element we were to mention, namely, Sympathy.

Of all helps given of God none is sweeter, more consoling, more strengthening, at times, than sympathy. There are seasons in life when it is to the soul what dew is to a parched and drooping flower. But sympathy is not open to all. It has limitations in its nature and exercise. In order to sympathize with a person you must possess the power to understand and appreciate the moods and thoughts of that person. A coarse nature cannot interpret the trials and experiences of a refined one. A practical mind cannot sympathize with an imaginative one. There are ranges of feeling peculiarly individual, at least peculiar to a class of individuals; and the hopes, yearnings, and trials which one heart may feel may be utterly unintelligible to another. Take birds as an illustration. They feed on different kinds of food: what one eats another rejects; what one recognizes as containing the elements its structure demands the other turns from as not belonging to its order of diet. Each has its own peculiar method of eating also. One will eat sitting on the limb of a tree, another floating on the surface of the water; while a third eats on the wing, searching the air for food, darting and wheeling this way and that, making the necessity of its lower organization minister to the exercise and amusement of its higher. So is it with men. There are many species in one intellectual and moral genus. The moral nature of one feeds on this, another on that. One class of minds gets growth and strength from what another class rejects as injurious. Thoughts and yearnings which are the daily food of one soul are fanciful, vain, and utterly incomprehensible to another.

Owing to this diversity of taste in people, it is not always possible to extend a healthful and grateful sympathy to one needing it. For you do not understand, and therefore cannot appreciate, the weakness, temperament, and trials of the person distressed. How often we encounter such cases! Their humors baffle us, their sayings bewilder us; we doubt the reality of their experiences, and deem their words flighty. But let this power to understand and appreciate your words and feelings be given one, — one whom when you meet him you instinctively know and feel understands you; to whom your words are not vague and senseless ramblings of mind; who can catch at your thought as a quick-witted person catches at a hint; who can put himself at your stand-point, and look at your life and troubles for a moment through your eyes; who, without having felt them, understands your feelings; who appreciates your errors and your virtues, sees your weak points and your strong ones; who is able to interpret yourself to yourself, and thus add to your inward knowledge; — such a person, and such a person alone, is able fully to sympathize with you. He understands you, and his knowledge is the medium through which he imparts his sympathy. Others may stand silent and powerless in the presence of your sorrow, but he is able to say the needed and comforting word. Others may misjudge you, but he is guided to the right conclusion by his sure analysis. His presence is a source of strength and moral inspiration to you. Around him the wings of your better life escape the vacuum, and find an atmosphere which they can beat, and on which they can rise.

I cannot but think that it was this faculty to understand and appreciate the nature and need of every human heart, finding infinite expression in Him, which so strongly and tenderly drew people toward Christ. He could sympathize with the publican because he saw in their true light the adverse social surroundings of the man, and the terrible strength of his temptations. Everybody seems to have been drawn to Christ. He magnetized people with the magnetism of His goodness. His character in its tenderness and completeness was a revelation. He was such to the fallen woman whom he saved from death at the hands of a brutal mob, and sent with tender exhortation from his presence. She had doubtless seen many good men, but never such a man as Christ. She had wickedly studied human nature on many sides, the better to practise her arts, perhaps; but here was a new revelation, and a phase of mercy she had never beheld. Over her swept the wave of a new and holy influence as He spoke to her. She felt for the first time that she was in the presence of One who knew her as she really was.

The very children loved Jesus. How could they help it? Do you think a perfect flower can command admiration, and the perfect Man of all the ages go unnoticed? Throngs followed Him whereever He went across the country, listening eagerly to His every word, and passing it from lip to lip. What a pity every word, every syllable, that He uttered could not have been reported and preserved! What a pity that this sole, this unique Man of all the generations of men could not have been presented to us in His every phase of speech, His every shade of thought! We only know that in Him was a wonderful charm, an inexpressible attractiveness. The Pharisees, it is true, hated Him; but they hated Him because they felt that He knew them, that He saw clearly through their hypocrisy and their cant.

Now I wish you all to feel, and to feel it in every drop of your blood to-night, that Christ as your friend sympathizes with you at all times and in all the moral conditions of your nature. Do not think that He sympathizes with you and loves you when in your best moods only; for if you should you would wrong Him bitterly. A bird is no more surely noted by the Father of all when, glancing upward through the morning light, he pours his liquid notes upon the fragrant air, than when, stricken by cruelty or evil chance, he lies fluttering, a bunch of ruffled and bloody plumage, upon the dewy lawn. And so it is with us, good friends. Our souls are not known and noted of God the most when, light and tuneful, they are lifted in ecstasy upward; but equally watched and as tenderly loved are we, when, stricken in hope, and soiled in spirit, we lie groaning and stunned, our purposes broken, our virtue stained, our future dark and forbidding.

Why, think of it! Do we love our loved ones only when they are strong and healthy and prosperous? Or is there something in weakness and sickness and adversity which draws from us a fuller and deeper tide of feeling toward those who are dependent on us? Say, mothers, do you love your children less when they are sick? Do you, father, yearn over your boy less when he is rebellious? I know your answer. There is something in love which survives all changes of condition, which keeps its growth long after the gray veil that no mortal hand may lift has fallen over the face of the wearied sleeper. But do you think that you can show a higher type of character than Christ? Are our hearts warmer, is our love truer, is our friendship more enduring, than the heart and love and friendship of the Lord Jesus? Who can say it? Who can think it?

But the peculiarity which most distinguishes friendship, and makes a friend so near and dear to us, is that it inspires one with the spirit of helpfulness. A friend means aid in time of need. In assistance cordially rendered he gives his feelings their proper expression. So essential and inherent is this sentiment to the very idea of friendship that you cannot conceive of the two being separated. You might as well attempt to conceive of day without light, or a stream without a current, as to try to picture friendship uninspired with such a motive. A person who would stand and lift no hand to your assistance when assistance was needed would forfeit in every one's estimation the title of friend. Not only at the moments of extreme necessity and peril, but also in the round of every-day life and experience, a friend serves you to the utmost of his power. When your ability is underrated, when your integrity is called in question, when your actions are misunderstood, and your words ignorantly or maliciously perverted, the voice and testimony of friendship are lifted in your defence. No person in business and professional life ever knows how many unselfishly and nobly are thus doing him service. No man knows how much the success of his life is owing to the strong current of approval started and continued in his favor by the unknown but efficient advocacy of his friends. Now and then it is given to one to ascertain the names and service of these friends; and many of you can bear witness that the names of those who spoke strong and brave words for you when strong and brave words were needed are never forgotten.

But, my hearers, it is unto Christ that you must look if you would see this the strongest and noblest element of friendship brought out in the clearest light. The friendship of Christ means assistance in the highest sense. He helps you by

His guidance and consolation on earth, and He will help you by His powerful advocacy when you stand before God in heaven. I trust none of us have lived altogether in vain; that our lives have not been altogether wrong, and that many on earth, and not a few in heaven, have cause to bless us. But we have also wrought wickedness at times. Our own consciences, imperfectly educated as they are, accuse us of sin; and what we need, what every one of you need, is a divine, a constant, sympathetic, and capable friend to plead our cause for us at the bar of God. If any atonement has been made to the transgressed law, if any equivalent to deserved penalty has been offered to Divine justice, whereby the condemnation can be lifted from my soul, then do I beseech that through the friendly offices of Christ it may be set to my account. I trust my case, otherwise hopeless, to the hands of the great Advocate, and have hope that His merits may make good my ill-desert.

I ask you to note the class and moral character of the people to whom Christ was a friend. The text says that He was a friend of "publicans and sinners," — that is, of those who are morally all wrong; whose very name and office had become a byword and synonyme of wickedness and evil thinking and evil doing. The Saviour I preach, as moved by the spirit of sincerity, and I trust of enlightened understanding, is a Saviour of men and women who are morally all out of the way. It is to you whose lives have been as it were a failure, whose natures, spiritually considered, are all in ruins, that Jesus comes in the spirit of friendly assistance to-night. You stand, it may be, amid broken purposes and overthrown resolutions and shivered hopes, and Christ, the great builder up of prostrated virtue, comes to your souls this evening, and, looking upon the ruin and waste which sin has caused, upon crushed hopes and buried expectations, says to you, "Come, let us clear away this rubbish, and, working in harmony, your will with mine, side by side, we will raise out of these fragments a structure of which the heavens shall not be ashamed." It is astonishing how far a little human material will go in such an undertaking under the supervision of Christ.

This is the spirit which pre-eminently characterizes Christianity. It is to the Gospel plan of salvation what the odor is to the flower, — the most subtile and exquisite expression of it. The very chiefest reason why Christianity has a right to claim your adherence is because she comes to you as a friend and assistant. She goes up to a man and says to him, "Here, you are having a hard time of it; let me help you." If he is blind, she says, "Give me your hand, I will lead and guide you." If disappointed, chafed, and despondent, she cries out cheerily to him, "Cheer up, friend, God never made such a being as you to despair." If suspicious, bitter, and cruel, she exclaims, "Why do you make a devil of yourself? You were not created to hate and hurt men, but to assist and bless them." If one is getting gross and heavy in his tendencies and tastes; if his mind is being polluted and his nature soiled; if appetite is getting the mastery over reason, she plants herself squarely before him, and shouts, "Why do you make a brute of yourself? Are you not ashamed to go into the gutter with swine? Come, wash and be more cleanly, and live as one of your make should live." This is the way religion helps a man. It helps him as a pruning-knife in a skilful hand helps a tree, — lopping off the dead, soggy branches, and pruning away the excrescences; not only so, — it helps him affirmatively as well as negatively. Where a vice had grown it inserts a virtue; where a thorn had protruded a blossom appears. The man thus gains in a double sense. He loses what tends toward death, and gains what adds to the development of his higher life. Piety is expansion. It does not cramp and fetter the nature. It enlarges and liberalizes it; shoots it out in all manner of new activities, and widens it with a thousand generous impulses. A small mean man cannot represent Christianity any more than a dwarf pear-tree can represent a forest. You must have some girth and altitude to you, if you would advertise religion. The church is not a treadmill, as some seem to regard it, where sad-featured men and women toil and tramp continually between set limits, longing to break loose and dash out, but are unable. It is a gymnasium rather, in which are vast appliances with which to exercise and develop the soul, and thereby add unto your nature a new vigor, a moral flexibility, a spiritual elasticity, in order that in the end (to continue the figure), when your grossness has been sweated off, and every power and faculty trained to the last degree of its capacity, you may be able, with death for your spring-board, to vault joyfully above the stars. The religion of Christ teaches a man that it is better to fly than to crawl; that virtue is sweeter than vice; that restraint is nobler than license; and that man, I care not how poor, weak, and erring he may be, may, by the grace of God, yet recover himself, and go to the grave with a hope in him that shall cause the portals of it to glow like the illuminated gateway of a palace when the king returns from battle, preceded by news of a glorious victory.

Let no one dare to preach, under the name of religion, a set of dry, juiceless dogmas to this generation, when men long to hear the glad news of human progress and human redemption. Every chord of my nature harmonizes with this popular note.

It is not theology, the science of God, so much as biology, the science of living, that I would impress upon you to-night. I would not, if I could, put any of you here into the strait-jackets of the schools. A man must be of stunted stock indeed, if he cannot grow so as to burst the lacings of any creed man ever devised. Creeds and formulas as the main-springs of Christian activity are of the past. They were born, undoubtedly, in part of the Spirit of God, but also in part of the spirit of human bigotry and bitterness and ignorance. The banner over us to-night, under which we are all marshalled, is not emblazoned with the name of Arminius, or Calvin, or Wesley, or Knox; but another name is on it, and the letters of fadeless light illuminate it from staff to border. It is the name by which God is known in heaven and on earth, — LOVE. The creed of a church is good for nothing save as it aids the church to better express its life and purpose and faith in Jesus Christ, and its yearning sympathy for man. The life which is yet to be lived ere our Lord and King shall come with His holy angels, marching visibly through the heavens in long and majestic processions of power, will not be inspired by the past, but by the future, — that future in which Jehovah yet veils Himself, patiently biding the hour for the perfect manifestation of His presence. The present, which some hastily call the hour of noonday glory, will appear to the ages ahead, when, teeming with life, they shall look backward upon it, as the dawn and twilight period of the church. Many a throne is to be levelled, many a system of error broken into fragments, ere the one throne and the perfect system of truth shall have been erected and inaugurated. The time is to be when God shall pour out His Spirit upon all flesh, and "your young men shall see visions, and your old men shall dream dreams." Then shall the Sun of Righteousness arise, full-orbed, resplendent with unshorn beams, every ray fulfilling its ministry of healing, and the light of it illuminating the earth from pole to pole. I live my life as a man whom every passing day brings nearer and nearer to fuller manifestations of God's power, to clearer exhibitions of the Spirit's energy, to a wider diffusion of Christian dispositions among mankind. The white and the black, the learned and the ignorant, shall yet stand together, angelic in their disposition and works, hand linked in hand, wing enfolding wing, in the unity of long-lost but acknowledged brotherhood, — the unity of perfect love. Draw, then, O men and women, your inspiration from the future. The air which drifts up from the past is heavy and dark with the mould and rank odor of ruins. Keep your faces turned fixedly and reverently ahead, and let the future, when the earth shall be full of the glory of the Lord, blow its perfumed breezes into your nostrils. Look and behold breaking through and scattering the mist of to-day the effulgence which streams upon you from to-morrow.

As I draw nigh to the closing words, let me speak to you directly of Christ. Let me lift, with a hand which will probably never lift it again before you all, the Cross of Calvary, — for that is the symbol of Christ's friendship for you, and the sole emblem of our fadeless hope. I would point you to the blood that was shed for you. I would repeat, ere my voice pass from your ears forever, the invitation and assurance of your ever-constant, ever-sympathetic, ever-helping Friend, — "Come unto me, all ye who are weary and heavy-laden, and I will give you rest." O woman, worn and bowed beneath cares and sorrows your laughing youth could not foresee, — O man, fretted and chafed, grimly enduring yet longing for rest, — and all you who stagger along your uneven paths, bearing up under failure and disappointment, and the load of your passions, with a bravery deserving a better cause and a better success, go and lay yourselves down under the shadow of the Rock. Lying there in humble dependence, the peace which passeth understanding shall descend upon you, as the dews of summer distil upon the earth, and you shall see, as Jacob in his dream of old time, angels ascending and descending, —

going up with your petition, and returning with supplies for all your needs.

As one who simulates no feeling, who never yet exaggerated his anxiety to supply his audience with a motive to act, who recognizes in the liberty he claims for his own mind the fullest liberty on the part of yours to decide, free from all outside pressure, this question of your immortal condition, — speaking thus, and in such a spirit, I urge you to no longer hesitate in what your reason and conscience tell you is right. Make and speak now that needed and noble resolution, which at many times of your life you have been on the point of making, but foolishly postponed. March no longer toward the grave as toward an enemy, but make your approach unto it as men journey toward the gateway of a palace, which, built at infinite cost, they have inherited in the line of royal succession.

I close with the thought, that, through the appropriated friendship of Christ, much which you have missed in this mortal life will be made up to you beyond the grave. In the gift of heaven is included all lesser gifts. Loves we have lost or barely missed, virtues we sought but might not attain, and the fulfilment of many a rudely interrupted dream, will greet us there. At death we shall have the opportunity to make a new start. We shall select and discard with a higher intelligence than guides us here. Beyond the grave we may not have the ordering of our lives, but we shall have great liberty in choosing, — even the liberty of the children of God. We shall be linked with whatever is most kindred to us in fibre and feeling, and streams widely apart on earth will converge in Christ, and, mingling, flow in union under that nightless sky forever. Many a blunder will be corrected, and many a failure made good there. I trust, good friends, that through the friendship of Christ, and our hearty acceptance of His assistance, it may chance that we shall meet in a temple far larger than this, not built by hands, and engage in purer worship with a numberless multitude beyond the skies, whose spaces, adorned of God, spread over our heads.

SERMON VIII.

HOPE FOR THE FALLEN.

"And the Lord said, Simon, Simon, behold, Satan hath desired to have you, that he may sift you as wheat: but I have prayed for thee that thy faith fail not; and when thou art converted, strengthen thy brethren." — LUKE xxii. 31, 32.

SOONER or later every Christian passes through a sifting process, — a process of temptation and trial, of failure and fall. The path which leads us to the beautiful gate is steep and rugged. No foot treads it far without faltering; no pilgrim enters the golden street with his sandals unworn; no head feels the blessed pressure of the crown which has not borne the markings of the thorn.

The words of our text introduce to your attention a disciple of Christ, when standing upon the brink of a great temptation, and a greater fall. He was about to be put under a pressure of which he did not dream. That pressure was to be too severe for him. He was to do a deed which will stand to his shame and humiliation, so long as the world endures. He was, as his Divine Master plainly said, about to be "sifted" by the Adversary.

There are two thoughts in connection with this text. I wish to suggest two lessons which I would impress upon your minds and hearts. The first is, the feeling of Christ toward Peter, and those who fall like Peter. The second is, the hope and duty of the fallen.

I would first, in order to expand the subject, call your attention to the clause, "I have prayed for thee."

You observe that the singular number of the pronoun is used. Of all the disciples who were to be sifted, or brought under temptation, it was to Peter alone that His heart went out in urgent entreaty. But why for Peter rather than for the others? Why should the merciful feelings of His heart be concentrated on him? Was it because he was nearer and dearer and more amiable than the others; more equitable in disposition, more exemplary and mild? No, for he was the reverse of this. Peter's eminence among the disciples at this time was not of this kind. He was hot-headed, rash, and egotistical, unstable and inconsistent. At one moment he was brave as a lion, heroic in all his impulses, and tense in all his purposes; the next he was timid, vacillating, and cowardly. You see him at one moment, sword in hand, foremost to defend his Master; the next he stands by the fire in the court-yard stamping and swearing, denying with oaths that he knew any such man as Jesus. But why should Christ pray for such a man? one is naturally led to inquire. Why did His love go out so warmly and tenderly toward one capable of so much treachery and falsehood, one so selfish and unreliable? Why select him from the other disciples, and lavish upon him so much tender solicitude and prayer?

Now, friends, learn what sort of a man Christ was, and what a moral phenomenon He was and is to the world. If you place your eye close to a hole in perforated paper, through an opening no larger than a pin's head you can see a landscape whose diameter is measured by miles, and whose limit is the limit of human vision. And so through this passage, when attentively considered, you will see how the nature of Christ unrolls itself; and the moral prospect the mind beholds is boundless and superlatively beautiful.

No, it was not because Peter was lovely and mild and consistent, but because he was just the reverse of all this, that Jesus prayed for him. It was not because he was strong and well braced, but because he was weak and liable to fall, that He remembered him. It was not because he was consistent and grave, and above suspicion — such as would make a good candidate for the deaconship to-day — that His heart yearned toward him, but because he was unsteady and fickle and notoriously reckless. I wish you all to observe here — for I know that it will comfort some of you — that the mercy of Christ abounds in the quality of discrimination. It adapts itself to man's needs, and flows according to the measure of those needs. I have heard it said that there is a law in nature by which the broken branch of the tree, and the bruised violet, and the wrenched shrub, and whatever else in the natural kingdom is maimed and hurt, draws the necessary elements of healing from the atmosphere; that the sun and wind and dew, the shadows that cool and the rays that warm, become physicians to it, and perform their free and unwearied ministries of love and healing. I have often thought how exactly this symbolized the nature of Christ and the operations of His love. Wherever you find a hurt or wound in the moral world, the healing influence of His love is drawn to it. Wherever you find a man wrenched and broken down in his hopes, — wherever you find a woman fallen and crushed, wherever a soul unstable and reckless, wherever any throe and agony, any crying and wrestling, any struggling and downfall, there Christ is. In thought not a few reverse this law. They forget that the love of God in its benevolent operations increases by the ratio of our needs, and that the lower down we are the stronger is the attraction which God centres upon us from above. At this point will doubtless occur to you all the cheering and infinitely tender words of Christ, when He said, "I came not to call the righteous but sinners to repentance"; and that other sentence, which carries with it the force of a demonstration,— "The whole need not a physician, but they that are sick."

Now men differ in blood and temper, in taste and feeling, as widely as in the build of their bodies and in the look of their faces. Now and then you meet a man or woman made as the birds are, to fly and sing. In all their inclinations, in all their propensities and aspirations, they are feathered and plumed for flight. There is little virtue, relatively considered, in some men being noble and generous, and some women being pure and gentle, because it requires little effort on their part to be thus. They were biassed toward such things at birth. They were dowered in their cradles with such qualities by their parents. And what a heritage it was! And how low and mean does any legacy of stocks and money appear beside it! Know and remember to-night that those parents who keep their bodies free from debasing appetites, and their minds uncontaminated by impure imaginations, shall, in bringing forth children like unto themselves, add beyond all other efforts of their lives to the bodily health and moral vigor of the world. I am fast coming to think that two thirds of every generation are mortgaged to the Devil before they are born, and that it takes twenty years of care and education to unrivet the fetters which, by their own lack of control and dissolute lives, the parents fasten on their children.

But, as I was saying, people differ. To some refinement is natural, and virtue easy. I have known women float through life as a white lily on a darkened stream, — beings of beauty and fragrance, buoyed up so airily by the natural encasements of their virtue, that not a drop or stain might touch or soil the exquisite whiteness of their souls. But others I have known that were like a lily, anchored by a law of its birth in a current, and it was swayed from side to side, and buffeted, and not a moment was there in which it was not threatened with submersion. Men, too, I have known, who were like granite columns, shapely, ponderous, immovable. Neither wind nor rain, no, nor the converging pressures of many wicked influences, could move them an inch. But others there are like reeds and rushes, weak and willowy, who cannot stand alone, but must stand in contact with and supported by many others, if they stand at all. Here is one that might seem almost a model, and you wish that all might be born like him. But anon you come across another, so weak and mean and effeminate that you wonder how he came to be born at all. He is a miraculous creation in an infinitesimal direction!

Times and seasons also make a vast difference with men in their moral relations.

Now there are seasons when, morally and socially, our experiences are as warm and genial and equitable as weather in early June, — when all our surroundings are fragrant, and the hours breezy with good news; when everything seems to be shaped for our comfort and prosperity; when health and credit are good, all our enterprises well-timed and successful, all our investments yielding good returns, and old debtors, from whom we had expected nothing, astonish us by their honesty. Now at such a time it is not difficult for a business-man to be good, any more than it is for a boy to sing or whistle when, with his fishing-rod over his shoulder, he goes with great swinging strides down the hill toward the trout-brook. There is no temptation for him to shorten or neglect family prayers, to be gruff to his wife or hard on his clerks, to drive his bargains to the very verge of dishonesty, to undermine his health by overwork, or commit suicide. When everything is prosperous and sunny, I say, a business-man has no temptation to be dishonest and unchristian.

But wait awhile. The season changes. June gives place to December. The sky gets black and squally. The wind veers, and, instead of coming like a warm, perfumed breath out of the south, it is poured in gusts and currents out of the north flecked with snow and dreary with sleet, which drenches the garments and chills through to the bone. Then is come the hour of weakness and trial. When credit sinks, and friends get suspicious, and investments yield nothing but loss, and the anxious brain carries its burden clean through the hours of sleep, and he rises unrefreshed, and failure stands not three days ahead of him, — this is the day and the hour when a business-man needs the assurance that, if there is sympathy for weakness in heaven, he has it. Many a man, as you know, has in such an hour closed his ledger with a groan, placed a pistol to his temples, and recklessly made for himself a blood-path out of his misfortunes or his shame. But I often think that the mercy of God is greater than some suppose, and that many a poor, harassed, crazed merchant, whose name is stricken in disgrace from the book of earthly exchange, will find it entered in the Lamb's book of life, and live to glorify forever the love which was greater than his guilt.

Now I want you to feel, all of you, that the mercy of God is full of discrimination in the time and measure of its outgoing. It goes out most strongly to the Peters of the world, and in the hour of their greatest temptations. God never leaves those who are in alliance with him to fight their battles alone. Ahead of you are temptations many, and struggles not a few. You will descend more than once to the arena and the assault, more than once be tempted to desert and deny your Lord; but strengthen yourselves with the thought that the heavens are prayerful for you. The Saviour foresees, as he foresaw in the case of Peter, how you are to be tried, and remembers you in his prayer. The prayer of Christ is worth more to man than weapon of steel or armor of brass. One word of intercession from Him avails beyond all our calling and crying. Yea, I could die mute and content, did I but know that my Saviour pleaded for me.

Now, as I have said, the future may be full of trial. There is nothing so black that it may not contain, — nothing so venomous but that it may lie coiled in it, ready to strike and fang you. But, fellow-Christians, let none of these things disturb you. Out of the future, out of its possible darkness and disaster, sound the strong, cheerful words of Christ, — "Ye believe in God, believe also in me." And the saints ready for the coffin check their feet on the borders of the grave for a moment, and, looking back toward us, with their faces already touched with the light of the eternal world, say, "Though we walk through the valley of the shadow of death, we will fear no evil; for God is with us,.His rod and His staff they comfort us." The living and the dying share equally in the discrimination of His mercy. To the weakest shall come the most strength, to the rashest the most control, to the neediest the most provision, and to the guiltiest the freest and most abundant pardon.

Now you see that Christ takes an interest in each of his disciples, even down to the most unworthy. Take our churches, and examine them in their individual membership. In them, as among the twelve, all shades of temper and degrees of consecration are represented. Here is a man who adorns his profession, and here another who barely escapes being a dishonor to Christ. Here a woman who, in the love of her children and the comforts of her home, finds all the security that earth affords, and the lively stimulus of a healthy pride. By her side, perhaps, sits another, torn we know not by what internal tumult wrought up day by day to an unnatural and ruinous excitement, and whirled around the circle of fashion so rapidly that more than once she has become dizzy, and spiritually lost her balance, and to-night she feels that she is in danger of repeating that fall.

Now there is, as I suspect, a feeling in our churches which leads men to overlook one of Christ's most lovely and beautiful characteristics. I refer to His solicitude for the wandering sheep of His fold. The feeling I have alluded to is this, — it is difficult to express it with precision in words, but I think I can give you my idea, — the feeling, I say, is this, that the consistent Christians monopolize, as it were, the attention and favor of Christ, to the exclusion of the delinquents. It is not regarded as credible that backsliders — the cold, the sluggish, and the dissolute — are recipients of His favor. His pride and joy in the ninety and nine orderly, safely housed, and well-behaved sheep, and not his anxiety for the wild, foolish, lost one, are for the most part the theme of thought and remark. And this unscriptural and complacent sentiment grows and grows, until a division line is drawn between the main body of the membership and the backslider as sharp, as cruelly defined, and as difficult to pass, as if the poor man or woman had actually been excommunicated.

Now this is all wrong, and yet the mental revolt which many of you may detect in your minds against what I am saying is the best of all gauges to show you how deeply rooted this idea has grown to be in the average judgment of the church. The Johns who repose on His bosom, and not the poor, hot-headed Peters, who stand stamping and swearing in the market-places, are the ones we deem the objects of His pity.

The practical evils which come from this idea are these, — it encourages spiritual pride and pharisaical complacency on the part of the majority of the church; it also substitutes another sentiment than that of love in our own hearts toward our backsliding brethren; and, lastly, it serves to plunge the delinquents themselves into a certain posture of antagonism to the church, and an inward despair touching their own ultimate betterment. This is the worst of all possible positions a man can get into. When the Devil has threaded all the hope out of a man, he has not merely cheated God of the first harvest, but has destroyed the very seeds from which all future fruitfulness was to come. Now, if there is a single man or woman here who is in or near the margin of such a state of mind, the lesson of this text is for him. He holds to the members of his church, more fortunate in temperament and training, the same relation that Peter held to the Twelve, when the words of our text were first spoken. He is the object of Christ's prayer to-day. My brother, I do not know how often or how far you may have fallen. No one save God does know. I do not care for that. Never shall it be said that ten years of Christian life have left me worse than a Pharisee. It is not in my heart to cast a stone at you. What have I to do with stoning? Perhaps for twenty years you have been unfaithful to your covenant vows, been derelict in duty, loved money more than Christ, been proud and vain, in all the plans and purposes of your heart worldly, in your appetites carnal. I do not know but that, since you were last in a sanctuary, you have in act and word denied your Master, as did Peter, nor can I see upon the border of what future denial your feet may even now be standing. I only know, my brother and sister, that Christ singles out, from all His disciples here, you who are most tempted and most liable to fall, and, going down to your side, as you sit in this hall, and fixing His eyes in love upon you, says, "I have prayed for thee, that thy faith fail not"; and all I ask of you is that you shall remember this, and go out from this place to-night girded and braced with the thought that Christ has not cast you off because of your sins, and turned you adrift, but that he sees all your weakness and liability to fall, and has singled you out from us all, not in anger, not to reject and thrust you away, but to assist and put his arms of loving restraint around you, and will so continue to do to your dying day. The words of Paul are true, — as true now as ever, as true to the modern church as to the church at Rome; and you should all be persuaded that neither life nor death, nor things present, nor things to come, nor anything that can happen to you, can separate you from God's love.

This is the anchor, the hope, to which I ask you to weld your faith. So rivet yourself to it to-night that when the next gale bears down upon you you will not be driven out of the harbor of your refuge, out of your confidence in Christ's redeeming blood, to be tossed and buffeted amid conflicting doubts and fears, but be held stoutly to your trust, as a ship is held to its anchorage when the anchor is struck into the cleft of a riven rock. There is not ahead of you a hand's-breadth of sky which is not of crimson, typical of a fair to-morrow, so long as in your heart lives a single regret for sin, and a deep, warm desire to be better; and out of that tinted, roseate sky come words of encouragement, and signs of promise, and unspoken messages, and ministrations of love and hope. And not only so, but that sky deepens and brightens its hue as it slopes downward; and at death, when Satan shall gather all his terrors, God will gather all His consolations, and that hour which so many paint with blackness shall be as radiant to the believer as golden mist. And all this I urge you to believe, not with wishing and a vague hope, but with the firm assurance of faith.

I would now call your attention to the last clause of the text, "When thou art converted, strengthen thy brethren."

Now if there is any class of men from whom the church popularly does not expect strength, it is pre-eminently from that class known as "back-sliders." If the mercy of God was like the charity of men, who of us would find forgiveness? If a professing Christian trips and falls, although it be far less in extent than the lapse of Peter, it is all over with him, so far as popular estimation goes.

No matter how useful he may have been. He may have preached the gospel, and labored with good results, for twenty years, but if caught off his guard for a moment, he is overpowered by the Adversary, and falls,— farewell to his usefulness. "*You* strengthen the brethren, indeed! Has it not been proved that you were intoxicated, that you were picked up drunk in the street, and lost your church by it? You are a likely person to preach righteousness and temperance and judgment to come!" Or again: "*You* exhort or pray again in public! Did you not forge a check, were you not tried for it, and barely escaped the prison, and did not your church excommunicate you for it? I would like to know what good your words and prayers would do!"

My friends, that is the way that the world, and the church, too, talks about men who have fallen; but it is a wretchedly sad way of talking, after all. If Peter had been a modern Christian, very slight chance indeed would have been his after that exhibition of himself in the court-yard. And yet there was a vast deal of noble, self-denying, soul-saving work in Peter after his terrible lapse from his Master, as you all know; for the Scriptures bear witness to it, and heaven is full of the testimony and praise of it to-night. And this Christ saw, for He laid a solemn charge upon him in these words, "When thou art converted, strengthen thy brethren." In saying this the Saviour enunciated one of the greatest principles known to the student of moral forces. The principle is this, — that all instruction and warning in spiritual matters must be based on knowledge and experience.

If I had a stretch of rapids to run, and could select from a dozen guides, I would choose that one who, when he last went down that terrible reach of water, at the point of the wildest whirl and loudest roar had his canoe twisted from the pressure of his paddle, sucked from under him, and crushed to fragments on the rocky bottom. And the reason would be, that he who once barely escaped death, when next he neared that point would approach with his senses all alert, and know to the width of an inch where to steer, and drive his flying shell straight to the proper point. And so it is on that other river which we call life, and along those portions of it where the current is swift and full of eddies, the decline steep, and the suction strong. He who has passed down such a passage, and been morally near wreck, is the man to caution and strengthen me for the danger. No one can talk to young men, for instance, concerning the woe of drunkenness like the reformed drunkard. Who can tell you of the horror of fire as he who comes staggering out of a burning building with his hands blistered, his hair burnt to the scalp, and the skin of his face puffed and white with the inflammation of the heat and steam? When that man talks about the torment of fire, you look at his face and see that he knows what fire is. Why, I might stand and advocate temperance, and you would listen respectfully, as becomes you, and that would be all. My words would make no great impression, start no new conviction, nor move any such emotion of pity or fear as you are capable of feeling. But let me bring a man here and place him before you who has been a drunkard, a city sot for ten years, and yet whom many of you would remember as an active and prosperous business-man fifteen years ago, a kind husband, a good citizen, and an upright gentleman. If I could bring such a man here, I say, and place him before you just as I found him in the street, ill clothed, tremulous and weak, would you not listen? As you saw his pale, haggard countenance, seamed and marred with the traces of debauch, — his eyes, out of which hunger and despair looked, — the shaking of his hand as he stretched it out toward you, — the broken-down condition of the whole man, — and out of his quivering lips heard the words: "I had a happy wife once, but my cruelty killed her. I had wealth, as some of you know, but rum took it from me. I had a home in that long-gone day, but the sheriff sold it over my head. I had hope once, both as to this world and the world to come, but the light of it has faded, for my days are passing in disgrace, and I know that no drunkard can inherit the kingdom of heaven!" and then heard him declare the truth extorted from him by his agony, "The wine-cup has done all this for me: beware of the wine-cup!" would you not be moved, seeing this man, hearing his words of warning? Would not the virtue of these young men be strengthened against the accursed drinking customs of the day? Well, this law holds good to a greater or less extent through all grades of experience, and none might be so useful to society and the church as those who have fallen, and by their falling gained the right and power to address intelligent counsel and warning to others.

God lays a mission, therefore, on all of you who by sad experience know the weakness of your own natures, and the readiness of God to forgive. It is to you who are wise with the knowledge of your weakness that I speak; to you who are in that unfortunate condition of mind in which a professor thinks that his past unfaithfulness cuts him off from any future attempts of usefulness, that I address the exhortation of the text. I know not where you worship. I do not know even your name. My arrow is drawn at a venture, winged only by the Spirit of God. But this makes no difference with my feelings or with our relations. For to-night, at least, I am your pastor; for to-night I am the voice of God to your soul. Hear me as such. Let your past be as a wild and frightful dream that comes in the night and torments us with its visions of terror, but departs with the rising of the sun. Forget your past. Your repentance has covered and changed it. Behold! see for yourselves! its scarlet has become like wool, and its crimson white as snow! Do not think that you are counted out of the moral influences of your church by its pastor? If he be a true under-shepherd of Christ, he lays on you the injunction that was laid upon Peter. There is not a summation he makes of the powers and forces to be organized in the future for Christ and man in which you, your wealth, your time, your friendship, your influence, your example, are not counted. So far as your past has been wasted you are to remedy it, and so live hereafter as to strengthen the brethren.

Why, see the philosophy of this thing. Suppose fifty men, who had lapsed from the perfect fulfilment of their covenant duties, and have been adding little to the moral forces of their respective localities, should say, not all at once perhaps, not in so many words, but in heart and act, "I have not been doing my duty to the church, no, nor to my own soul either, and I will change my course, rectify my example, and henceforth, God helping me, will be faithful to my pledge," — would not that strengthen the brethren? Who can estimate the power of such a stand, the addition which such a confession and reconsecration would bring to the spiritual forces there? And the farther the man had wandered, the more marked his failure in the past, the more noticeable and influential for good would be his return to duty.

Return, then, return, all ye who have wandered! Come back, ye prodigals, smitten with spiritual famine, to your Father's love and home! Let your clerks, let your servants, let your children, let your pastor, see the blessed change in your conduct. Behold! into this audience the Spirit is now entering. He comes as the wind to the orchard when about to bloom. What memories of former activity, what resolutions for usefulness, what hopes of future labors, sweeter than the perfume of flowers, are stirred as His impulse sways your minds! O, blow upon us, thou Divine wind! Come to these frozen hearts here, as the warm air of the south comes to the ice in spring, melting it! Come to these darkened minds, as a breeze comes out of the west after a day of storm, sweeping the clouds from the firmament, uncovering its majestic vault of garnished blue! Come, as the scented zephyr to the lattice of the sick! Come, as hope comes to the lost, as faith to the dying, and as that eternal peace which the world knoweth not comes to the sainted dead! Behold, we lift our eyes and hands and hearts, and say, "Thou Holy Spirit, come!"

SERMON IX.

THE MINISTRY OF THE WORD.

"Preach the Word." — 2 TIMOTHY iv. 2.

NOTHING is more evident than this, — that the death of Christ neither wrought any change in the feelings of God toward the sinner, nor in the feelings of the sinner toward God. Whatever the atonement did effect, whatever use it served, it certainly did not modify the relative status of either. From the beginning God had loved man with an infinite love. To that there could not come, by any occurrence, addition. From the fall of our first parents through all their successive generations, their moral alienation and antagonism remained, and after Christ had wrought out and finished his great work on earth and reascended into heaven, human nature remained in all its old state of lapse and degeneracy.

From the start there had been two obstacles to man's salvation. The first was that which the just and holy claim of the transgressed law presented. God must ever remain harmonious with Himself. He cannot favor one attribute at the expense of another. His justice must be satisfied before mercy can be exercised. In the Divine economy the death of Christ sufficed to meet the demand of the law. It was a perfect satisfaction to justice. In its legal connection it was held as a full and ample equivalent of the punishment of the sinner. Divine justice was honored, and without discordance to Himself God could allow the sentiment of His mercy exercise. After the death of Christ God could justify the unjust, and yet remain just to Himself. Thus the first great obstacle to man's salvation was removed. But no sooner was the first obstacle removed than the second presented itself, namely, How might the enmity of the human heart to the plan of salvation itself be removed? The death of Christ opened, if I might so express it, a broad, macadamized road along which the feet of men might pass, without let or hindrance of justice, heavenward; and the cross, planted as a guide and sign at the entrance of it, sent out its impressive and perpetual exhortation to all to enter, — but none would enter. A road, I say, was opened; a path, wide and smooth, rising with easy grade upward, lay before the race; a highway, at infinite cost, had been cast up, along which the nations in long and happy procession might tread; when — surprising fatuity! — a discovery was made, — the nations would not walk in it! An astonishing and persistent disinclination to be saved on the part of the imperilled, revealed itself. The avenue remained untraversed by the very ones for whose benefit it had been opened. The possibility of freedom had no sooner been proclaimed to those in spiritual slavery than it was discovered that, instead of appreciating the privilege, instead of eagerly availing themselves of the chance of liberty and restoration, they absolutely preferred their bondage. They gazed with unlighted eyes at the Cross, which was the sign and seal of the government's love and care for them, and heard the proclamation of hope and redemption from their chains without one emotion of gratitude, and even with ignorant and defiant murmurs. What was to be done? Leave them to toil and die in this base condition, or educate them up to an appreciation of their privileges? You anticipate the answer. God never despairs, never halts in His merciful undertakings. In the flow of His love lie the infinite resources of cleansing. No pollution discourages Him. He is to sin what the sun is to darkness, — its master by inherent composition of forces. The second obstacle in the way of men's salvation — their disinclination to be saved — did not appall Him. He proceeded at once to devise and set in operation means for its removal. He commissioned agents, and organized agencies; the object of all their influence was to overcome the sinner's disinclination to be saved. In this we find the origin and motive of the ministry of the Word.

By the ministry of the Word I do not, of course, mean that part of it alone expressed by the preacher, but all those enlightening, convincing, and convicting influences which flow from the history and revelation of God's dealings with man. This book is indeed the source and head of the Christian ministry and Christian influence, but it does not give full expression to that ministry and influence, any more than the spring in the mountain gives full expression to the river, of which it is the beginning and first cause. Consider how many books the Bible has given birth to, and what a vast influence those books have exerted and are now exerting on the human mind. Reflect, furthermore, how literature has been cleansed and modified by it; and how the poetic imaginations of the race, purified from heathenish conceptions and lewdness, are to-day busily at work swelling the aggregate of virtue and refinement. Where, indeed, has not the influence of the Word penetrated? Where has not the ministry of it, in one form or another, gone? It has entered into literature, and purged it of its indecencies and grossness. It has directed the chisel of the sculptor, and made the marble contribute to its holiest conceptions. It has mingled the colors on the palette, and endowed the canvas with a perpetual power to refine and elevate. It has dictated constitutions to governments; wrenched legalized wrong out of statute, and marshalled the forces of legislation in favor of liberty and man. It has even entered the seat of customs, made commerce an honor and an agent, and joined in close alliance with itself all the manifold forces of business and trade. It is only when you take into account all these wide-branching influences which emanate from the Bible, that you can, even to a partial extent, estimate what it has done and is doing for the world. Now the ministry of the Word, which has for its object the removal of man's hostility to God, in its widest sense, includes all these. By as much as you enlighten the race, by as much as you refine away its grossness, by as much as you root out its vices and extract its antagonisms, by so much do you bring it nigher to God. The early rains which precede the summer's warmth do no more surely prepare the earth for the seed, than do these world-wide, humanizing tendencies, which through a lengthened pedigree trace their birth from the Gospels, prepare the souls of men to accept the atonement. There are, I have no doubt, men and women in this audience to-night who have been thus indirectly operated upon by the Spirit, until you stand as orchards do in June when ready to break into floral beauty and fragrance as soon as the warm southwest shall blow upon them. You are at the very point of presenting yourselves to God with every faculty in full bloom. Through a literature which the Gospels have purged and made clean, — through home influences, which are the gift of the Cross to the nations that embrace it, — through the providential dealings of life and death, — through manifold methods, your minds have been enlightened, your consciences quickened, your hearts made tender; and, to-night, you are as the soil when the sower passes over it with the seed. God grant that the truth may find lodgement to-night in those hearts best prepared for its coming, for so shall it spring up, blossom, and bear fruit after its kind.

I do not want you who have not as yet recorded your love for God to feel that the Sabbath is the only time, or the church the only place, or clergymen the only men, when, where, and by whom the ministry of the Word is proclaimed. The descent of the Spirit is like the distillation of dew, — not confined to the hours of one night, but yielded by the heavens under the workings of an organic law of mercy. Wherever you find discipline for your passions, wherever control over your appetites, wherever food and exercise for your virtue, wherever opportunity for benevolent action, — whenever or wherever a sight of beauty or sound of harmony, or anything of God or man sweet, pure, and elevating, then and there are you ministered unto out of infinite mercy. Then and there does God seek to take you, as a gardener does a vine which has been wrenched away from the trellis, and with the tenderest touch and solicitude train you once more around the prop and pillar of Divine support. There is such a thing as narrowing religion and its offices by the way in which you regard them. Some look at the ministry as I was wont to amuse myself when a boy by looking at objects through a glass with the ends reversed; and the result is that they see but one man, — and what a small one he often appears to be! My friends, the minister of the Word is not the ministry of it. The one may be very small. He is but a man at the best; but the other is vast, full of expansion,— a combination of forces powerful and not a few, of whose action and energy God himself is the motive cause. The minister is a man, with the weaknesses, foibles, and imperfections of a man. His appearance may not please you, his manners and habits of thought and speech may offend you. Pique, prejudice, and a superior taste may all combine to make you dislike him. But the ministry of the Word, who can dislike that? What taste can criticise sunlight? What refinement take offence at the solar warmth? The sense of smell might as soon cry out against fragrance as man's soul revolt at the sweet ministries of God's love. Now I feel that I am speaking to men who know much of life, to men whose work it is to build dams in swift currents, whose very business puts them under daily pressure and temptation; and I wish you all to feel that the ministry of God's Word comes to you through many channels beside my voice. The anchor of your hope, friends, is not cast within any church, but within the veil, which is the presence of God; and your daily words and acts strengthen or sever the strands of which the cable that connects you therewith is woven. God ministers to you in ways manifold, and methods not a few, — in the crash of your overthrown fortunes cloven by an unexpected bolt; in the wreck of your worldly plans and hopes; in the family altar, or the mournful absence of it; in the habit of caution and prudence which your dealings with men have taught you; in the dying and burying you behold; in the privileges of liberty, and the powers and pleasures of knowledge that you enjoy. All these are but the methods of His ministry to you. These are the electrified wires along which His messages of warning and direction come. These are His angels, commissioned of His mercy, and whose mouths are full of entreaties higher and more impressive than man's. No! My voice is but for a moment. It sounds, and the sound of it passes away forever. The moment that you pass from these doors to-night you plunge again into a current, — the current of worldly life and business, the current of temptation to cheat and deceive, and put a price upon your virtue. And I know well that in the roar of that stream my words will be lost, and the sound of their warning be drowned. Yea, and if God shall not then minister to you in some other way, and brace you up, you will be spun from off your feet and swept down stream. But God's love is like the sun, and it rays its warmth and light along many lines, and its illumination is everywhere. You cannot escape from it any of you. It will be with you in the week to come, yea, and through all the weeks of your lives; and they will be sweetened by the ministries of it, as meadows are sweetened by the fragrance of many flowers, seen and unseen, — now a breath rising at your very feet, and anon another and a sweeter blown to you from afar.

Now I would that you all might feel this, because it is truth, and also might recognize with most devout gratitude to-night the source of it. All those ministrations calculated to soften, refine, and lift you come from God through Christ. Every drop in this broad river on which the world, and especially this nation, floats like a richly freighted ship, has come down to us from Calvary. Over the very fountain-head of all these outflowing influences the Cross stands, and will stand forever as the symbol and sign. And it is because of the love of God to us that our feet stand in such high and privileged places to-day, where we overlook such an auspicious future.

Now it is possible that some of you have fallen, for it is natural for men and women to trip. You stand to-day like those who have entered many races, but never have won in any, — discouraged, spiritless, or in a kind of sullen despair. Now I wish all of you who are in any sense in such a condition of mind to cheer up and enter once more. Make one more attempt. Nerve yourselves for a vigorous effort. The eyes of the brave look forever into azure, the eyes of the coward forever into blackness. If I could single out that one who has made a greater failure of his life than the majority of us, whose future morally is black, who has reached that lowest state in which a man can stand, — when temptation has only to present itself and he instantly yields to it, — who is regarded with sorrow and displeasure by the church, and with suspicion or contempt by the world, I would go to him and say, "My good fellow, cheer up. There is a chance in your future yet." Why, I went down to the scene of a conflagration one day, — marked by a heap of ruins from which smoke and steam were still issuing. What a power there is in fire! No wonder that it is used in Scripture as a symbol of hell. What terror there is in the rush and roar of it! What suggestions of stifling, as it whirls a blast of hot air into your face! What a parent of eddyings and whirlwinds its fierce heat is! How it sucks and roars and flares and shoots its columns of red flame upward, as the current which itself has created draws through it! For terror and power and suggestions of peril, which make men spring from their beds, and women shriek, and children scream, what can compare with fire? Well, this terrible agent had been at work at that warehouse; it had beaten down the roofs, and pushed over the walls, and dashed down its supports, and broken all its massive braces, and left literally nothing but masses of bent and half-molten iron, the foundation-stones, and the bare earth on which they rested. There never was a more complete ruin, never a more total overthrow. Twelve months after I stood on that corner again. I looked about me bewildered. I crossed the street, and gazed wonderingly upward. Could I believe the evidence of my senses? The ruins had disappeared, every trace of fire was gone, and a massive structure of granite and iron towered nigh to a hundred feet above my head; and the spacious compartments resounded with the whir of wheels, the creaking of pulleys, and the shouting of men trundling bales and straining at the elevators. And I said to myself: "Man is indomitable. No failure discourages, no wreck appalls him. From the ashes of his old the creation of his new conceptions arise, and the failure of yesterday gives birth to the triumph of to-day."

But do you think, good friends, that material ruins are the only ones men can rebuild? Is the destruction of warehouses and mansions the sole destruction he can remedy? Are the prostrated columns of trade the only ones he can re-raise and establish? I tell you nay; the same resolution, the same energy, the same hopefulness and effort, carried into the sphere of moral disaster and wreck, will accomplish even more glorious results. I care not what or how much has been overthrown. Honesty, virtue, sobriety, — all may have gone down, but so long as the foundation, which is life, is left, so long is there hope and opportunity. So I say to you all, no matter what may have been your failure, nor how total your overthrow, — no matter, spiritually, where you stand to-day, nor how black and ugly is the face of the past as it scowls at you through your recollections, — you are not lost, you are not undone, you need not despair. You have only to clear away the rubbish from the foundation, and begin again. In this endeavor you will not work alone. There is not a twig on a tree which seeks growth, there is not a flower in the field that craves fragrance, unassisted of God. But are you not of more value in His sight than flowers and trees? Does the sun withhold its rays from a bruised violet which a thoughtless foot has crushed? Do the clouds refuse to condense themselves above the parched ground, and empty from their distended borders the moisture of the shower? Does not the solar beam slant an equal ray upon the mud of your streets and the grass of your lawns? And if God is thus mindful through nature to minister to the inanimate and the senseless, will He be less thoughtful and loving in His provisions for you? Never believe it. You will be ministered to, you will be fed; yea, as young birds, blind to the mouth that feeds them, so the providence of God, moving on noiseless wing, will come laden with nourishment, and perch above you, silencing your clamors by supply; and all that is pure and noble in you shall be grown and developed under the brooding love of God, until at the breaking of some bright morning the hour of flight and song will come, and you will never have done with soaring and singing.

I have dwelt thus at length on the ministrations of the Word as a means to remove man's opposition to God, that you might see how nigh in manifold methods your Heavenly Father comes to you in your daily life. I wish all you business-men, and all you young men, and all you laborers here, to feel that God's truth is not shut up between the covers of any book, nor proclaimed by any man or class of men alone, but that you may find and feel it anywhere and at all times; that day by day it comes knocking at the door of your hearts seeking entrance. The influence of the Spirit which inclines us toward Christ is not enclosed in pipe-like ordinances and formulas, and led into our churches as you enclose and lead water into your reservoirs. No! It is, rather, like the water which flows in the river, permeating the earth on either side with its irrigation. It lurks like moisture in the atmosphere, and sifts from the heavens like dew, or falls on human hearts as the outpoured shower upon the thirsty soil in summer. This Divine influence is as universal as atmosphere, as generic to the moral order and economy of God as sunshine is to the material world. Your souls are not like birds in a vacuum, which fall plump to the bottom of the jar, and lie gasping and fluttering, unable to lift themselves. They are, rather, as those same birds when in the free outer air, under the curvature of whose wings a strong current of wind is sweeping, and all they need is to poise correctly with easiest inclination this way and that, and the movement beneath lifts them. What a sight it is to see a bird thus suspended above you, and to watch him as he poises with nicest balance, while the invisible but adequate forces under him push him upward until he seems but a tuft of brilliant plumage smitten by the sun! So it is, spiritually, with you all. You do not lie gasping in a morally thin and exhausted atmosphere. You breathe an air full of the bracing element of noble impulses. Underneath you are the uplifting influences of God's Spirit, coursing steady and strong like the wind. I ask you to-night to put yourselves in such a position that you can be lifted. I do not address you as professors or non-professors, as penitent or hardened. I speak as to men and women endowed with reason, gifted with sensibilities to feel, capable of gratitude, able to decide as to what is right and just. I place heaven before you in these closing words. You can see, if you will but look, the streets and walls and gates, and all the outflashing glories of it. You know what a force the Cross is in the world; why it was set up, and what forgiveness of sin and impulses toward virtue men receive from it. I ask why so many of you reject it. Is there not a tide of conviction setting many of you toward it? I feel it to be so. Do not resist, do not struggle against it. Steer directly and joyfully toward it, rather, as ships long buffeted by storm come flying in from the foam and thunder of the tempest-swept ocean toward the protection of the harbor and the quiet waters of the bay.

Suppose, my hearers, that this city should yield itself, in the action of all its inhabitants, to the ministrations of God. Suppose the men who conduct its business, build its houses, swarm its factories, people its streets, and direct its energies, should in the coming week, by the grace of God, be converted, and ever after bear the name and live the life of Christians. What mind here can adequately conceive of the blessed change such an event would cause? What absence of vice, what peace, what prosperity, what hope, would be ours! And yet such a result would be brought about by individual decisions. Though all were converted at the same moment, yet each of you would have to decide for yourself. Why should it not begin here in this room, to-night? Who of you will be the first to decide? Quick, for the heavens are watching! Whose is the name that goes first into the skies?

O the decisions of this night! Better by far to have stayed away than, having come, to decide wrongly! If, as it is said, the fall of a pebble shakes the earth to its centre, how heaven vibrates with the thoughts you are thinking now! To think and not to conclude; to conclude only to decide amiss; to add one more grief to the sorrows of the Spirit, one more rejection to the many you have already given to Christ, one more insult to God; to do this, moreover, on the Sabbath evening, God's own day, set apart by Him for your especial benefit, bringing to you such an opportunity, being, as it may be, your last on earth — ah, who can bear the thought?

Enough has been spoken, — too much if it be in vain. I turn from the shadow to the sunshine, from the clouds and fogs of the present to the pure azure of the future. The banners under which I ask you to serve to-night will yet be blazoned with victory. They will shake out their glory over the heads of those whose feet will enter heaven as the feet of those who are more than conquerors. Decide as you may, God's purposes will not change. Whether you contend or assist, His cause will move on with the motion of a chariot when a king drives it to victory. Over thrones and proud empires the Nazarene has walked, on shield and pennon his feet have trodden; and to-day, amid the kingdoms of the earth, He marches on, the centre of agencies more destructive than cannon, more terrible than an army with banners. Think you that the cause of which Christ is the leader will fail of complete vindication? Will the influences of which He is parent, which have braved successfully all manner of opposition for so many centuries, which have levelled so many palaces, overturned so many thrones, broken so many fetters, enlightened so many minds, ever die? It cannot be. We shall go to our graves, fellow-Christians, but we shall go as warriors have gone who lived long enough to know that their bravery was not in vain. We shall sleep, not as those who have no hope, but as they who hear far down the future the smiting of victorious shields and the shoutings of a great multitude. Amid the tumult and commotions of the earth, amid the roar of all battles, the Christian hears but one voice, publishing itself with the sustained clearness of a bugle, saying only this, but saying it forever, "Behold, I make all things new." And God who is over all shall minister unto all, until this Divine assurance shall have been fulfilled.

I invoke the Spirit of Christianity. From her birthplace in the East, with the flush of the Orient yet kindling on her brow, I summon her to the West. I invoke her presence in your hearts, in your homes, throughout all your streets. Under her inspiration may you live, and by the winged mercies of it be at last lifted into the skies. For so will it come about that you will die easily when you come to die, and put your arms around the pillars of Death, not with fear and shrinking, but as those who find that they have arrived at a happy opportunity.

SERMON X.

THE CHURCH, — ITS OBJECT AND CAPACITY.

"And so were the churches established in the faith, and increased in number daily." — ACTS xvi. 5.

THE subject I propose to discuss before you this evening is this, — The Christian Church, its Object and Capacity. My more immediate desire is to examine into the status of the Church as it now exists, and the character of public sentiment toward it.

The Church, in its universal application, signifies the aggregate body of believers in Christ, — faith in Christ, as a Redeemer from sin, being the distinctive characteristic of those who compose it; and all who believe in Christ as the Saviour, whatever may be their views touching interpretation and minor doctrines, are its members. This is the general meaning of the term.

In a local sense, a church is composed of any number of Christian believers who, from feelings of duty to God, each other, and the world, have consociated for mutual profit, and that they may the better advance the kingdom of God. The Church, originated in Christ as the Pastor, and the twelve disciples as the original members. It was continued and multiplied by apostolic authority and labors, and has been constantly identified with all that concerns the advancement of God's spiritual kingdom.

It should also be observed that the conviction of all Christians, up to a very recent date, has from age to age most positively reaffirmed the Divine origin and sufficiency of the Church. The current of Christian sentiment has set, I say, with an uninterrupted flow in this direction,— that in the local churches, in the powers and functions, the agents and agencies, they represented, the world recognized an institution not merely begun in Christ, but all-sufficient to accomplish, so far as human instrumentalities can, the work of Christ on the earth. This, I repeat, has been, up to a recent period, beyond question the universal sentiment of Christians. The great impulse given to missionary effort, near the beginning of this century, which resulted in the establishment of the Foreign Board and Home Missionary societies, had as its prime cause this idea,— that Christ held His Church responsible for the conversion of the world. And it is this thought, ever present in the bosom of the local churches, which to-day holds them steadily up to the line of consecrated endeavor. This I regard a fair statement.

Now there are two opinions, growing apace, hostile to this view of the Church. Neither is as yet fully developed; one not sufficiently confident to express itself in words. But unless one of these opinions is checked and the other corrected, we shall soon see them both in the field in open and undisguised opposition to the Church. What at present is only whispered in the ear will be proclaimed from the housetops, and an embarrassing and grievous schism will occur, the result of which no one can foresee. I will here present more fully both of these opinions, hostile as they are to the scriptural and hitherto universally accepted view of the uses and objects of the Church, — show whence in part they arise, what is their tendency, and how to render them powerless for harm.

The first opinion is this: That the Church, although originally an excellent institution, and one which in time past has served moral interests, is now outgrown and left behind by the progress of events, and through the operation of its own past benevolent action has become useless and effete.

They who hold to this opinion are men and women of sceptical and so-called liberal tendencies of mind, — people of radical and erratic temperaments, who by nature are inclined to reject and override whatever offers the least restraint to their latest-formed opinion or speculation. Many of this class have been checked and balked in what, it must be confessed, were most noble endeavors for human advancement, by the slow and cautious movements of the Church, or perhaps still more by its direct and persistent opposition; and they have naturally, looking at it from their point of view, jumped to the conclusion that the Church is a cumbrous and uninspired organization, which has no sympathy with human wants, and is opposed to all needed change; and which, through its laws, ordinances, and ceremonies, and above all through its vast hold on human credulity and unintelligent reverence, blocks up by an unrequired machinery the path of just and salutary reform. They instance the attitude of the churches toward the antislavery cause in the early stages of its history, their present lethargy touching the temperance movement, the unwise and unspiritual conduct of the Presbyterian and Episcopal denominations in reference to those of their members who are most active in labors of love and efforts to give the Gospels free scope; and charge that, practically and in point of fact, the Church prevents the accomplishment of the objects for which it was originally ordained. Furthermore, they inveigh against the spirit of caste and exclusiveness which exists in the Church, shown chiefly in the construction of magnificent palaces of worship for the few, while the many have not the Word of God preached to them, and charge that even its activities are thus proved to be in opposition to the evangelization of the masses. They also urge that there is in the churches such blind adherence to old forms and customs, which every sensible person knows are practically of no value in our day, — such timidity and conservatism in its worst sense, — such bigotry and intolerance manifested in their refusal to receive, any to their fellowship who cannot intellectually subscribe to their covenants and human interpretation of Scripture, — such opposition to science, which it thereby forces into antagonism to the Bible, — that no enlightened, philanthropic, and progressive persons can conscientiously belong to them; and hence such must work outside, if at all, of their iron-like and ever-contracting circumference. They also declare that no latitude, no freedom of thought, no liberty of investigation, is allowed the preacher or members; that the fear, nay, the certainty of discipline and excommunication with the accompanying loss of reputation and forfeiture of confidence and support, is held over their heads, and hence no reform can ever come to existing evils, because the very sources of reform — free discussion and investigation — are things denied. I might instance other charges; but these, in substance, make up the grave indictment against the Church as an institution.

Here, then, is a charge, held, made, and discussed openly and by many. Some of the cleverest writers of the country are weekly, in one form or another, reiterating it. Some of the ablest speakers are proclaiming it, now in the form of argument, now of satire, now of invective. Some of the best men and women of the land — if money given, if time devoted, if life consecrated to human good are to be admitted as testimony of character — are believing it. And it is to be feared that numbers are tacit disciples of the doctrine, whom timidity, interest, or lack of occasion and prominence unite to keep silent.

Now, my friends, you will observe that the strength of this charge lies, not in the ability of the makers of it, nor in their persistence and honesty, although these are powerful elements of persuasion in this country, but in the fact that there is a certain amount of truth in the charge itself. The indictment is strong and to be dreaded, I say, because the party against whom it is drawn is in a measure guilty. It is true that the position of the American churches in relation to the antislavery reform, tested either by the votes of their presbyteries and consociations, by the voice of their pulpits, or the votes of the membership, was not in harmony with the spirit of the Gospel, or with a correct and humane public opinion. When Mr. Garrison went to the prominent clergymen of this city, begging that they would assume the leadership of a cause to guide which he felt himself, young and unknown as he was, to be incompetent, and was rebuffed by all, —

even the elder Beecher turning him off with the proverb, "I have too many irons already in the fire, young man, to attend to it," he did by that act expose the spiritual deadness and unscriptural position of the churches. When a Presbyterian synod excommunicates one of its most godly and energetic members, because he will sing songs other than the psalms of David,—good soul-lifting Methodist hymns, and those tunes which make the Sabbath-school melodies so refreshing, — it gives cause for Piety itself to arraign it. When the Episcopal Church arrogates to itself to say that Mr. Tyng shall not preach Jesus Christ to dying men, unless in surplice, and a building consecrated by a bishop's invocation, it puts a weapon into every hand hostile to the Church as a divinely organized and soul-converting institution. It makes possible and just the charge, that professed followers of the Saviour bar and ban the free and benevolent flow of redeeming grace. When any church forbids a man of intelligence and veracity, who claims to love the Lord Jesus as his Saviour, to enter its communion; shutting his devout and hungering soul away from the table of his Lord, from the broken bread and symbolic wine, because of some intellectual difference of opinion touching some minor doctrine, or some little matter of detail touching the government of his life, which are subjects of pastoral conference and instruction, and not evidence of repentance and faith,—it does by that act not merely expose itself to the charge of intolerance, but offends one of Christ's "little ones," and in so doing pains the Saviour Himself. Many a professed Christian, also, by the manner in which he has treated his spiritual teacher; by an unfriendly watching his public utterances in order to detect some doctrinal unsoundness, or to catch him in some verbal lapse in what his own narrow and ignorant mind had conceived to be orthodox; by dwelling upon and publishing the discoveries of his suspiciousness; by helping thus to perpetuate a public opinion opposed to growth in knowledge and therefore in grace;—many a professed Christian, I say, has by such conduct filled the quiver of satire with the arrows, and forged for invective the bolts, at the launching forth of which the bosom of the Church has been lacerated, and the honor of her enjoyed and royal liberty in Christ prostrated.

No; the Church is not free from blame in these particulars. She has more than once taken positions that have made her obnoxious to a just censure. She has shared in the world's selfishness and cruelty, and set herself against what she afterwards acknowledged was of God's own doing; and to-day she is by no means impregnable to a criticism the severity of which lies in the fact that it is just. This is, then, the first source of that distrust of and opposition to the Church as an institution which one who watches events and the tendencies of the times sees is beginning to assert itself.

Now, friends, how can this feeling be checked? How can we prevent this sentiment from going on and extending itself indefinitely? How can we take those elements out of the atmosphere which, if allowed to multiply and combine, will in some evil hour descend with the velocity and violence of lightning upon the organization that we love, and in which we believe the hope of the world lies?

Well, I know of but one way. It is this: The churches must, henceforth, so act as to make criticism powerless. "When is criticism powerless?" you inquire. "When it is palpably unjust," I respond. This every public man in the country knows from his own experience. The sentiment of fair-play, of equity between man and man, is pre-eminent in America. The Anglo-Saxon is the only race with which the jury system has ever been a success; where, indeed, it has ever been seriously attempted. In no other country are public men so fiercely assailed as in this; in no other are they so safe, provided that in the main they are right. No one man, no clique of men, not even a newspaper, can lie a man out of usefulness in this country. They may pile falsehood upon falsehood against him, they may cover him with abuse, they may pervert his words and malign his motives, they may task the utmost resource of misrepresentation to his hurt; but the American people will hear both sides before they render judgment. Every public man knows this. It is the joy and safeguard of public life. Stanton knew it. Lincoln knew it. Beecher leans confidently upon that belief to-day. You may pass this as a maxim,—no one can be condemned in this country on malicious reports, on mere hearsay. Criticism, in order to be powerful, to be hurtful in America, must be just. In the long run, every man and every institution gets its deserts.

Well, by this star should the Church be guided. We must put the Church in such a position toward man in all his needs, toward society in all its wants, that adverse criticism will have nothing reasonable to hurl against it. We must so act that any but malicious opposition will be impossible, and therefore harmless. Our love for man, our labors for his best interest, must be so open, so self-evident, so like the sky at noonday, that no eye can fail to see and rejoice at it; so that even the blind shall bless the warmth of that beneficent influence the source of which they cannot in their blindness behold. The safety of the Church lies in progress. It cannot become an intrenched camp. You can never so fortify it that the world will not storm over its walls, and leave it, as an army leaves an enemy's city, a mass of ruins. The Church is not a walled city, it is a movable column, and its safety lies in moving on continually. Those who anchor it to one fixed position, who would wall it in with formulas and moat it round with orders and creeds, are its worst foes. If the Church does not lead the race, the race will walk over the Church, and go on without it. Human advancement will not stop for any institution whatever. If any one should be foolish enough to array the Church against science, do you think science will stop? If any against reform, think you reforms will cease? Nay, you must annihilate mind before you can check the progress of science. You must root out sympathy and humane impulse and divinely inspired love from the soul, ere man will tamely surrender his inalienable right to expand and elevate himself and his kind. The prerogative of immortality will be given up only with the soul's consciousness.

The second source of peril to the Church, the second sentiment that is hostile to it, lies, not in the opposition of outsiders, but in the scepticism of a portion of its membership as to its powers and capabilities.

Like the other, this feeling is in an undeveloped state. It is latent, or in its first stage of manifestation. Many do not suspect its existence, when in fact it has already become a part of their conviction. As in the case of insanity, the acts, and not the consciousness, of the patient reveal the lapse of reason; so the actions, rather than the sensation, of many in the Church testify to the lapsed state of their views and feelings concerning the powers and destiny of the Church.

The feeling, I say, is evidently growing in the Church that the Church is not sufficient in and of itself to convert the world; that some other organization must be raised up in order to reach the mass of men with the saving truth of the Gospel. Only a few weeks ago a young man, eminent in the religious world, expresed to me the conviction that the Church was destined to decline and give place to other organizations, until, at the coming of Christ, there would be no Church. He based his belief on the assumption that the Church was unable to meet the exigencies of the future. For years there has been a growing inclination to work outside of the churches, as it is styled; to build up other organizations, and make them independent of the churches. The idea has gone abroad, and lacks not advocates in private conversation and public conventions, that the churches are not adequate to the work; that they are too unwieldy and inelastic to accomplish what the Master requires to be done; that they answer the wants of a certain upper class of society, are admirable as educational institutions, but powerless to reach the masses; unfitted, for instance, to do the work of searching out and assisting young men in our cities; not qualified for the rough, wide-awake, hand-to-hand work of converting souls. There is not a person of intelligence in this audience who does not know that this feeling is abroad and being expressed in manifold ways.

Now I have this to say at the outset: If the Church is not sufficient to carry forward the Master's cause, then something must be raised up that is. The cause must go on, Church or no Church. Souls must be converted, and if the Church is not able, is not adapted, to do the work, then must it go by the board. No obstruction must be tolerated to men's salvation; no half-and-half institution permitted to retard, even for a day, God's saving purposes of grace.

The question, therefore, comes squarely before us, — and the more thorough the discussion the more satisfactory will be the conclusion that the public will reach, — Is the Church, as an organization, able to go ahead and meet the obligations of the future, or must it be given up as a converting agent, and some other raised up to do the Lord's work? This, when stripped of all merely accidental considerations, is the real proposition. For to say that the Church is to be retained when the accomplishment of the great object for which it was organized is to be left to other hands borders on the ridiculous.

The idea that the Church is in the years ahead to be nothing but an educational institution, or a convenient agent for administering the sacraments, while all the active, soul-saving work is to be done outside of it, — all the zealous, consecrated workers to be beyond its direction and control, — is an idea which has in it, should it ever gain popular ascendency, force enough to destroy the Church and wipe it out entirely.

My friends, you can regard this as certain, — the Church can never exist disconnected with active, aggressive conversion work. It was never formed for a mere educational and sacramental institution, and can never continue as such. There can be no such thing as a church outside of a membership; and when the active, working men and women who compose the Church, and make it a vital and vitalizing power, array themselves under other banners and names, the Church will cease to exist as a body or become paralyzed in influence. Its membership is to it what the breath is to the nostrils, and with the breath life departs. So then it is safe to say, that if the Church is not to live as a converting power and agent, it cannot live at all.

I call your attention, furthermore, to the thought, that the real force of this query, — what makes it dangerous to the Church, — is to be found in the fact that it is raised in the Church itself. It is not an assault from without; it is a revolt (I use the word in a modified sense) from within. The query has been started in the very circle of Christ's disciples. It is a hesitation, a wavering, a losing of heart, a desertion amid His own followers, and those followers, too, upon whom He has most relied. The divergence, amounting in some localities almost to a schism, is, I say, within the Church itself, and the fair structure of her spiritual unity is liable to be rent asunder. There are certain phrases and expressions uttered in conventions, and going the round of the press, that serve to gauge the extent of this sentiment.

Now, friends, bear in mind that words are symbols of ideas. They hold the same relation to our feelings as letters do to thought. As clouds reveal to the eye the motion of invisible atmospheric currents, so words show the drift and direction of otherwise undiscovered opinions. Words are teachers also. They educate a people. They are to ideas what colporteurs are to tracts, — they disseminate them from house to house. Words are missionaries of the brain; tireless servants they are, that voyage over all seas, climb all mountains, penetrate the deepest valleys, drawn as by an irresistible attraction wherever there is an eye to see, an ear to hear, or a brain to understand. Launch a word out upon the air, charged with the propelling energy of an idea, and who shall set limits to its flight? who tell where it will stop?

The world of mind will never let such a word perish. Its pilgrimage is endless, and it will traverse the entire realm of thought and impulse. Like the wandering Jew, its footprints will be found on the shore where the equatorial ocean rolls its heated waves upon the hotter sands; in the snows of the far north the traveller will see them by the polar light, and where, as the ancients held, the sun cools the flaming wheels of his chariot in the western tide, — wherever man is, there will that word be, impressing men's minds, shaping their opinions, and serving the cause which sent it out commissioned as its herald. What men say is an index of what men think, and he who would know what public opinion will be to-morrow must note carefully the public utterances of to-day.

The phrases to which I allude, and which I use to show the drift of opinion as represented by some men, are these and the like. They say, in speaking of the Young Men's Christian Associations, for instance, "They help the churches," "They have done so or so for the churches," "They are in close sympathy and alliance with the churches." What would you think of a man who should talk about the Sabbath school "helping the church," or the Mission school as having done this or that for the church, or the prayer-meeting as being in "close alliance" with the church? Why, the Sabbath school is the church as truly as the preaching service. The Mission school and the prayer-meeting are the church. These are not outside, independent organizations any more than the ministry is an outside, independent organization. They are no more separate from the Church than apples are from the tree on whose branches they hang. From bulbous to ripened state the Church fed them, and all the life, all the vitality, all the sweetness they have is derived from the blood and breast of their grand old nursing Mother. The foot has as good a right to separate itself from the limb, or the limbs from the body, and call themselves independent organizations, and talk patronizingly of the trunk, as the several co-ordinate branches of the Church have to separate themselves from her, and start off into independency. They are all members of one body, of which Christ is the regnant Head. So long as they remain in Christ they are indivisible. They compose one organic unity. The clasp of an indissoluble union is around them. He who holds and teaches any other doctrine opens wide the door of possible difference, antagonism, and feud.

Now, if you search for the origin of this sentiment, of this doubt and scepticism touching the Church, its powers and capacity, you find that it is a stream that has two sources, — one of which is the lethargy of the Church. The Church, as an organization, failed to meet the requirements of the age, failed to improve the openings of Divine providence, failed to supply the more active portion of her membership with work. Active, benevolent natures tire of forms and ceremonies; their souls instinctively reject such dry husks, and clamor for richer food. They cannot be content with a dull, insipid routine of experience; they cannot see men lost without making an effort to save them. The churches, partly from egotism, partly from timidity, failed to change their administration so as to meet the wants of the times,—failed to enlarge the sphere of their activities, failed to bestir themselves for the salvation of the multitudes. The result was, that the zealous portion of their membership, especially the younger, finding no opportunity to work inside the churches, feeling itself repressed, fettered, intimidated, broke away from their direction and control, and struck out for themselves. If they could not work in the Church, they would work out of it,—for work they must. The long-repressed, accumulating, pent-up water, finding no sufficient outlet through the ecclesiastical flume, broke over and swept away the traditional dam, and flowed whithersoever it would. This current of heaven-inspired impulse, which should have been utilized in the churches, was gathered into another organization, and the Young Men's Christian Association was the result. Unemployed in the churches, the young men naturally jumped to the conclusion that the churches could not furnish them work, and this is now, I fear, fast ripening into the conviction that God never intended that they should. Hence the expression, "We help the churches," "We are in close alliance with the churches," — which phrases mark as clearly as words can, not a lack of love for the churches (the movement has not reached that stage yet), but a scepticism as to the capacity of the Church, as an organization, to furnish employment to its members, and a practical divorcement and separation from it. That is one of the two causes alluded to.

Another cause is to be joined to this; the mingling of the two, — what may be termed the duplex cause, — makes the problem intricate.

It is, as you know, in the nature of every organization to enlarge, solidify, and protect itself, and the more successful an organization the stronger does this tendency become, until at last it grows to be the prime incentive, the controlling impulse, and what was accidental and looked upon as a temporary expedient becomes confirmed and takes the position of permanency. Personal energy, not entirely free from a questionable ambition, assumption of superior excellence, and a sensitiveness quick to resent friendly suggestion as a hostile criticism, — these and other elements of power go to swell the total of the tendency in question. This is the law. A hundred illustrations from history might be brought to prove it. Indeed, the best possible illustration is being day by day given in our midst; and many who little think it, will at no remote period, unless wisdom prevails, be called upon to decide whether the Church of Christ or another organization — an organization which at its inception was designed to be no more separate, no more independent of the Church than the Sabbath school or prayer-meeting — shall receive their presence and their labors. For when the churches shall lift themselves, as they are sure to do, to an acknowledgement of the wants of the age, and their manifest duty; when they shall reeve in all their sails, and spread them to catch the rising breeze of opportunity; when every hand and every eye is needed to work the ship, then will a voice go forth calling the wandering crews aboard; then must the gayly painted and newly launched yachts be left, that the ships of God may sail full manned whither the one sure Pilot may direct and the wind-like Spirit waft them.

I have thus, friends, frankly discussed before you the two sentiments that are hostile to the Church, — shown you the origin of each, and how you can make both powerless for harm. For one, I regard the Church as above all human institutions. Its history is unique and sublime. Having for its foundation the words and deeds, the life and death, of the One Man, it has stood the shocks of time without being overthrown. Its walls are not of granite, yet have they stood when granite has crumbled. Marble and porphyry and bronze have yielded to time, but the passage of years has served only to confirm and strengthen the organization of God. Upon the Church the Adversary has tried his every art, and exhausted his utmost fury. The fagot and rack, exile and death, have all been used, time and again, to break the cordon of believing hearts united by faith in Christ; but no assault of fire or sword has severed it. Without her ministrations the Word of God would have been an unread and unknown book. In her have been generated and grown those benevolent energies which have elevated and blessed mankind, and which to-day, with tireless zeal, are carrying the Gospel to every desert tribe and the savage islands of the seas. She needs no eulogy from any. I borrow out of God's free air no breath, I marshal no words of stirring speech, to sound her praise. Her wreath is woven, and well woven too, both flower and leaf. Let no one tell me of another organization that is to supplant the Church of the Most High. Let no one tell me that her arm is shortened or her knees weak. Say not that there is, or can ever be, an altar like hers, moistened as it is with the blood of her martyrs, and smoking as it does with the incense of her praise. Others may seek new houses and strange temples, but the house of the Lord, the sanctuary of the Most High, shall be my spiritual home. I am content with the glory of the Church, I am satisfied with her praise; for the beams of her house are of cedar, and her rafters of fir.

SERMON XI.

THE POWER OF CITIES.

FROM the earliest period to the present time cities have dominated over the world. Into them have flowed the resources of national power. In their hands have been held the balance of empire, and the human mind has ever acknowledged the sovereignty of their sway.

Paris is France. That phrase has passed into a proverb. In it all that is light and beautiful in the French character, all that is wild and violent, all that is poetic and refined, all that is gross and sensual, is represented. The very gossip of its boulevards epitomizes the philosophy of the nation. It is the heart of the empire, and every province sympathizes with the action of its great centre. If Paris is satisfied, the empire is peace; if the capital is convulsed, the nation quakes to its remotest boundary. In this wonderful city the valor, the culture, the science, the poetry, and religion of the Gallic mind are concentrated. More than once has the judgment of the nation against its kings been expressed in the savage roar of the *canaille*. More than once has French liberty been smothered in the blood of its streets, and hope entombed beneath the ruins of the barricades.

Rome is Italy. Garibaldi saw it first, and strove to burst its gates for the entrance of Italian nationality with the rush of his volunteers. Cavour, the only statesman Italy — I had almost said the only statesman Europe — has had for a century, until Bismarck appeared, — Cavour saw it next, and attempted by diplomacy what the hero of revolution has failed to accomplish with the rifle and the sword. He died in the midst of his labors, his plans yet unconsummated; and Italy stands to-day like a body without a head. Her natural capital, the city which most nobly represents her past, so fitted to express her future, is in foreign and hostile hands. Nevertheless, the adage is correct, — Rome is Italy.

If I should allude to the past, your minds would more readily yet catch the opening thought of this discourse, and realize the potent influence wielded by cities on national morals and life.

Jerusalem, whether ablaze with the glory of golden tiles, as in the time of Solomon, or with all her magnificence buried beneath the ruins of her walls and the *débris* of the Temple, as during the captivity, — at whatever date or in whatever condition you beheld her, she was Jerusalem still, and being Jerusalem, represented the Jews. The poetry, the piety, the bigotry, the glory and shame, of the

Hebrew race were all enclosed within the circuit of her walls. Here they crowned their kings, stoned their prophets, and held their feasts. Here the harp of the Poet King sounded its melodious prophecies of the Messiah's birth, and here that Messiah received His sentence and His death. To the Jew there was but one city, as there was but one temple, in all the world. The power and glory of the Jewish name were enclosed within the city of his home and heart.

But why enumerate? You are familiar with history. Why speak of Thebes with her hundred gates, through which power radiated to the remotest corner of her domain; of Carthage, that swarthy rival of Old Rome, which dominated over the Afric coast; of Alexandria, city of books, into which the lore of the whole world had been gathered; of Tyre and Sidon, marvels of wickedness, associated with and begotten of wealth, such as the world had never seen, the sails of whose ships were of silk, and through whose streets floated the odors of every clime; or of those vast cities, each city an empire in itself, that stood along the banks of the many-mouthed Nile; or of Rome herself, to whose consuls the whole world, marching along the Appian Way, brought tribute? All these are known to you. The history of the human race has been but the history of cities. Their rise and fall, their progression and declension, are to the race what the ebb and flood of the tide are to the sea. They have been the *thesauri* of the world's treasuries. The ingenuity and skill, the industry and perseverance, the valor and cowardice, the virtue and sin, the life and death, of each successive generation have found expression in them. They have been the oracles of human wisdom, the monuments of human greatness, the arsenals of human power. Whether you study their rise, existence, or their fall, they epitomize the knowledge of the race and the results of human effort.

It would be interesting, had we the time, to examine into the causes which underlie the origin of cities, and trace out the mental, social, and material agencies to which their erection is due. It would be found, could we push our inquiries in this direction, that each of these had contributed its full share to the common result. By nature men are gregarious; they flock together. The spirit of combination is as old as the race. Were the story of the building of Babel but a myth, it would still be pregnant with instruction. That attempt, that first gigantic association of human endeavor, whether a fact or a fable, would still stand as a grand expression of a profound impulse, the embodiment of a primal idea. That embodiment by the wisdom and power of God was checked, the agents and agencies scattered; but the idea, the causal impulse remained, and does remain up to this day. While the race endures, the same tendency will prevail; the same spirit of combination will receive the identical expression. The confusion of tongues cannot check it. Application overcomes the obstacle of diverse languages. The antagonism of speech can be harmonized, and the chaos of unintelligible sounds reduced to order. As the natural result of our social and mental construction, strengthened by considerations of interest, cities will continue to be builded; Art will seek some central galleries in which to exhibit her achievements; Eloquence will build a platform from which to address the multitude; Architecture will chisel its granite and mass its structures in imposing conjunction; Commerce, inspired with the instinct of trade, will land her cargoes at accessible and central points. Men, from a natural tendency in part, from material necessity in part, will herd and mass together, even to their own detriment, and cities will be built. The future will be as the past. The causes which have existed will exist only more abundantly, and the history of the centuries to come, as of the centuries passed, will be the history of their cities.

If you will take a map of the North American continent, as you behold the length of its seacoast, its capacious harbors, the multitude of its navigable rivers, some of them almost bisecting the country, furnishing an inland communication unrivalled in the world; the vast extent and location of its great lakes; the position of certain localities, which makes them both the reservoir and outlet for the products of the adjacent country,—you will be led to exclaim, "This is to be a nation of cities." The very conformation of the coast compels us to this conclusion, and even declares where they shall be built. Take New York as an illustration: a city which reigns queen of a continent,—a city with an island for her throne, and ships for her messengers; who delighteth herself with the cry of her pilots, and to whose feet the waves of either ocean wash the wealth of the world. Search for her origin. Her parentage was not of men. Her conception was of old time, when the Almighty traced the boundary of the sea. She was begotten with the primal pangs of nature, when this continent came forth from the womb of waters. New York is the child of God, born when He drew the outlines of our shores; plighted to commerce and all its growth, when He placed her in the arms of two rivers, and breathed life into her by the cool breath of the ocean. Men, indeed, have clothed her in satin and adorned her with gold, but she was begotten out of the sea by the Spirit of the Lord. Consider the conformation of the coast, behold the vast extent of territory to which she is the natural outlet, and you see at a glance, that, granted a civilized and industrious population back of Manhattan Island, and a city at that point is a commercial necessity. And to-day, with all her wealth and prestige, how long would New York endure if the Hand which opened should close the outlet to the ocean, and sever that great artery which connects her by way of the lakes with the heart of the continent?

All that I have said touching New York is equally true of Boston. Upon the shore of Massachusetts Bay, so soon as New England should become populous, a city would be sure to rise. The instinct of Trade would naturally select this site as the centre of her efforts and her success. Here piers would be builded and warehouses erected. Here, following in the train of wealth, mansions would successively rise. To this point art would be attracted, and here, in the leisure which money can purchase, letters would flourish, and every principle of science, in the necessities of your yearly growth, find substantial expression.

You may go west, along the shores of the great lakes and the banks of its majestic rivers, and you will find that the same law holds good. Even beyond the present limits of population, it is not difficult to locate those points where, as the restless multitude spreads itself over the plains, cities will spring up, and great central depots of wealth and power be established. Considering the energy of our people, the natural tendency and natural necessity of combination in all human undertakings, — considering the position and conformation of the continent, it is not hazardous to predict that this is pre-eminently to be a nation of cities. The Atlantic slope is already urban, and the time is not far distant when the valley of the Mississippi will rival, in the number and magnificence of its cities, the valleys of the Nile and the Euphrates, when the civilization and glory of the East were in their meridian glory.

Consider, now, the importance of cities as a source of influence.

If this reasoning is correct, if cities are to multiply and abound, you will see that the whole complexion of our future is to take color and character from this fact. The character of the people, the character of our institutions, is to be vastly affected thereby. There is a certain influence, a certain atmosphere in city life, which modifies and shapes, not only the speech and manners, but the thoughts and opinions, of men greatly. New England character is different to-day from what it was fifty years ago, because New England life is different now from what it was formerly. And this change in the life, in the thoughts, manners, and opinions of New England men and women has been brought about chiefly, as I believe, through the influence of our cities. Some of you, doubtless, can remember when the country influence preponderated in Massachusetts; when the wealth of the State was more equally divided between the urban and rural population than it is now; when in religion, in politics, in trade, in jurisprudence, the towns and villages of the State held the heaviest side of the balance; when the cities leaned, as it were, on the country, and felt their dependence upon it. You have lived to see all this changed; you yourselves have aided to change it. The cities have broken away from their dependence on the country, and the country now depends on them. The cities now dictate to the towns and villages. Through their great dailies they dictate in politics; through their pulpits, benevolent organizations, religious newspapers, and publishing-houses they originate and express the moral convictions of the churches; through their markets, their importers, their bank establishments, their stock exchanges, they dictate financially to the country; through art, æsthetically; through architecture they shape the farmer's house; through horticulture and landscape-gardening they are improving the appearance of every village and increasing the value of every farm. The telegraph, the rail-car, and every invention whereby the facilities of locomotion have been increased, and personal transit from place to place made cheap and easy, have all assisted to bring about and hasten this transformation. We have already reached that point of progress in this direction that it can be in very truth said that there is no country; in its old sense it does not exist. The country tavern and stage-coach have no more surely passed away than the old modes of thought, ideas, and character-forming habits have departed. City influence, city views, city customs, preponderate everywhere, and are destined to do so more and more.

I say that this change, this influence, will go on. Its present momentum alone insures it. Every sign points in this direction. The future will be cast in this mould. The nation will be more and more deeply stamped with this impress.

Consider the attractive power of cities. They draw the country population towards them by their magnetism. They are like huge sponges; they absorb the talent, the enterprise, the ambition, of every community that they touch with their power and influence. Estimate the number of young men in Boston to-day that were born outside the city's limits. I asked seven one day whence they came. Every one of them had come from Maine. Three out of the next five I met were born in New Hampshire. I took these twelve hap-hazard from my acquaintance. Take New York City. That city is a vast intellectual reservoir which drains half of New England, and would all of New Jersey were it not too sluggish to run! It has passed into an adage, that "no active, ambitious young man stays in the country." He sets his face toward a city, as a devotee of Mahomet sets his face toward Mecca. It is very easy to complain of this. It is fashionable to denounce it. Political economists may declare that the foundation of all wealth, the basis of all true national development, is agriculture; but neither regret nor economic demonstration will stop this great tidal movement of our population toward our cities. The laws which regulate such popular movements are beyond our control. Regret will never modify them. They will continue to operate and influence until some counter-attraction shall arise to neutralize them. Cities will multiply, cities will continue more and more to absorb the country, cities will eventually dictate the policy of the nation.

Here our feet press the threshold of the labyrinthine problem which, in the providence of God, we are called upon to penetrate and solve. Here we stand under the shadow of one of the great ominous questions of the future. The gravest question of our day — that which will tax and puzzle us most, and yet one which challenges us to instant and painstaking inquiry — is this, What is, and what is to be, the moral position and character of our cities? Can we safely trust them in respect to our liberties? Can we safely trust them in respect to religion? In those two propositions is wrapped up the destiny of the Republic and of the American Church. Will the Republic be secure? Will the Church be equal to the emergency? Here is ground for men of all creeds, of all opinions, of all pursuits and trades, to stand upon in common, to cordially strike hands in harmony of heart and action.

Well, consider this question a moment in its relation to the Republic.

If the Republic stands for anything, it stands not only as an expression of civil liberty, but for that which insures and guarantees this. When you discuss the continuance of the Republic, you discuss the continuance of law and order, and of public morality in all its various phases of growth and propagation. If the Republic means anything, it means a pure and upright judiciary, an active and untainted police administration, a well-protected industry, a well-observed Sabbath, a strictly guarded and untampered ballot-box, and a system of public education unsoiled with the touch of venal politics. These are to our free institutions what the roots are to the tree, — the channels of their growth, the braces of their power. When these are severed, when these are torn up and displaced, the vital currents cease to enter the trunk, the leaves wither, and the whole elaborate organization hastens to decay. If the Republic, in all the phases of its life and expression, cannot stand

and thrive in the soil and atmosphere of our cities, then, unless those cities undergo a change for the better, the time will surely come when the Republic will not stand at all. It will fall, and find its burial amid the fragments of its own once glorious structure. Its monument will be the ruins of its own overthrow.

Now what is the condition of our principal cities, politically, to-day? Look at New York, — a vast and almost bottomless cesspool of corruption, a dead weight of ignorance and venality, which the whole Empire State can with difficulty buoy up! Look at its judiciary, heavy with the murk of Tammany Hall, — a reproach to American Justice throughout the world! Look at its financial jugglery and shameful monopolies, at the expense of the nation and people! Recall that it owes even its police protection to the State. There has not been a time in twenty years when the suffrage of our greatest and, in some respects, our grandest city has not been two to one against every principle of justice and morality which underlies our free institutions; when the Republic would have stood an hour left to the voice of its decision. It is safe to say that Republicanism in New York City is a dead failure. The majority of its population are as hostile to the very elements of American Liberty and the Declaration of Independence as ignorance and venality and brutal viciousness can be.

You may go to Baltimore, to New Orleans, to St. Louis, and even to Chicago, and you will find such a state of morals, such a perverted judiciary, such disregard of the Sabbath, that, if permitted to grow, will soon rank them in wickedness with the great Babylon of America. You may take, for instance, the influence of cities on the several State legislatures. You let a few millionnaires come together and form what is called a "ring," and what a pressure they can and do put upon legislation! Measures opposed to every principle of public justice, bills creating and perpetuating monopolies which drain the best blood out of the industry of the State, are pushed through in the very teeth of all the opposition which a knowledge of their evil character and remaining virtue can heave up in their path. The outrage upon public sentiment and the true interests of the commonwealth is done openly, defiantly, unblushingly. But you should remember that this ill-omened influence, this startling phenomenon of power, originating and directed by pure selfishness, is yet in its infancy. It is but recently that it has entered as one of the elements of that problem which, under God, we are to work out on the shores of this continent. If already its strength is so considerable, what may we expect it to be when it shall have had time to grow and mature, and enter the lists against public morality and public interest in all the might of its fully developed manhood, equipped at every point?

Now consider for a moment the position of cities in reference to religion.

At the first thought, when you consider the number and variety of our church edifices, standing along almost every street and around our squares, you would exclaim, "What a religious city this is! how completely the population must be reached by the influence of the Gospel! how universal is the privilege of the sanctuary! how thorough and general the Sabbath-school education!" From this cursory view of things, one might conclude that all the families of the city must be church-goers, all the children religiously instructed, and every soul reached by the ministrations of the Gospel. But upon examination he would ascertain how erroneous such a conclusion is. He would discover that here, in Boston itself, vast multitudes never even enter a church; that hordes of children swarm the streets as wild and untaught as if Boston was a heathen city; that the churches, instead of gaining upon the inrolling tides of ignorance and superstition, do not even hold their own; that their seating capacity is not half equal to the necessities of the population, and, worse than all, not over half of the sittings provided are ordinarily occupied. And as these ugly facts thrust themselves upon his consciousness, he would be prompted to say, as some have said of late, "Protestantism is a failure." Well, there is a false and there is a true side to that statement. In its spirit, in its capacity to reach and elevate, in its destiny and ultimate issue, Protestantism is not and cannot be a failure. In it is light enough to illumine all the darkness of ignorance, and warmth enough to evaporate the dank vices which make so large a portion of our cities a moral marsh, a breeding-place of corruption. But in its present state of expression, measured by those it has not reached, — by the ignorance burrowing at the very doors of its churches, by the blinded eyes its fingers have never touched, by the naked it has never clothed, by those in prison it has never visited, by the souls in peril it has never saved nor made any attempt to save, — Protestantism in our principal cities is a failure. Neither the Republic nor Christianity could stand on the vote of our cities. Left to their suffrage, justice would become a mockery, liberty degenerate to license, and the Sabbath sink to a mere holiday.

The failure of the Protestant Church to realize her relation to the masses has been and is her chiefest error, so far as Christianizing the world goes. We have hitherto cultivated the table-lands of society; we must now drain the marshes and uplift the swamp level, by running purifying channels through their oozy beds. From these rise those moral miasmas which carry taint and contagion to the very mountain-top of our civilization. A Spiritual Board of Health must be formed, and heavenly disinfectants be applied to every damp lane and filthy tenement of our cities. We must run our fingers under the very roots of society, and transplant it bodily into a drier and warmer soil. This is not pleasant work. It is a tiresome and hand-soiling horticulture. The fragrance of the rose and the orange is not in it. Broad walks and wide lawns and the cooling shadow of trees do not invite and relieve the laborer. Nothing short of the pressure of clearly apprehended duty will sustain one in it. Easier by far is it to give charities than to distribute them; to provide bandages than to bind up the bleeding wounds. And yet the work must be done, or the world will never be brought to the knowledge and the practice of Christian precepts.

Now it is just this, the personality of well-doing, that I would place before you in this condition. As Christians, benevolently disposed, we should individualize our benevolence. It is not for the condition of the race at large that we are so responsible as for those individual members of the race that are near us. I am not so anxious for the Christianization of Pekin and Calcutta as I am for the Christianization of Boston. It is the ignorance here I would enlighten, and the misery here I would alleviate. I do not blush for the heathenism of China so much as for the heathenism of North Street. I do not fear the cannibal of the South Seas so much as I do the drunkards and gamblers and Sabbath-breakers at our very doors. It is not over some Rome or far-distant barbarian city that I lament; it is over this Jerusalem of New England, this Mecca of the Republic, that I mourn. When we reflect how much the United States is to influence the world, and that as a nation we are growing to be more and more influenced by our cities, the improvement of their moral condition becomes the great question of the day, — a question which must be debated and settled speedily. I would that all the churches of this city, of all creeds or without creeds, might meet in solemn convention, to unite and fix upon some plan by which, with the power of combined resources, they might carry personal cleanliness and comfort, good food and raiment, education and the glad news of Redemption, to the dirty, the starving, the vicious and ignorant portion of our population. I believe that a movement might be inaugurated by which all the moral and humane influences of this city might be combined in furtherance of so blessed an undertaking. I know well that sectarian and denominational differences, that strong prejudices and some bitter memories, stand in the way; but when vice and squalor burrow under the very thresholds of our churches, when thousands live within sight of our steeples to whom the Sabbath has no meaning, and Christ is an unknown word, save to point a jest or emphasize an oath, it is not the time for us to ask men, in order to find a point of difference, "What do you believe?" but, that we may ascertain some sure ground of union, "What are you willing to do?" We must address ourselves to this question, or else our church-steeples will seem to the multitude but cruel mockeries, and the volume of our prayers be drowned in the torrent of their cursing.

I need not tell you how natural it is for men to exaggerate the value of forms and formulas. You know the lesson of history and the warning of Christ: we are to walk by the Spirit, not alone by the letter. We are to believe only that we may act. Faith is not the end. Pertinacious adherence to a creed, however true, is not holiness. It was not the beautiful beatitudes of Christ, nor the Sermon on the Mount, nor His farewell to His disciples,—which, as an expression of undying love, has no equal in literature, — it was His blood which saved us, by making atonement for our sins. It was what He did, not what He said, that liquidated Heaven's vast claim against us. And so, my friends, it is not our prayers and hymns, our words and thoughts and hopes, which meet the claim of duty now being put upon us; it is by well-doing, not by well-saying or believing, that we can discharge the requirements of the hour. For one, and I say it gladly, whoever will work for Christ and man, let him come to my side, and he shall be to me as a brother. Not by his creed nor by his church; not by his form of prayer, but by his works, will I know him. Not by the bark, nor the leaves, nor the shape of the trunk, but by the fruit, shall the tree be judged. Let the churches, let all the Christian men and women unite; let the humane and religious portion of our population bury their past differences, cease from invective and useless discussion of each other's peculiar form of belief, and join hands to ameliorate the condition of the poor and ignorant of the city. While we wrangle over theological beliefs, the suffering and neglected die.

As I walk the streets of our city, where vice makes its retreats, and poverty crouches in rags to conceal its nakedness; as I think of the fingers that bleed from ill-paid toil, and the eyes that ache; as I behold the swarms of children that must be rescued from the condition into which they were born, or perish, — Arabs of the street, and candidates for the gallows, from whom your prisons are fed, and the army of crime, already fearfully large in this country, receives its annual reinforcement; — as I behold these, I say, and think of their destiny, I feel that even a Hindoo would be welcome, could he aid me to save them from their fate. O the patience of God, that He can bear with our idling and listlessness! that He can look calmly on and see us debate trivial differences, and elevate our prejudices to the dignity of essentials, while thousands on thousands living all about us are at this moment without God and without hope in the world! I marvel that He does not shake the heavens in angry warning over our heads, or visit us with some calamity, — some terrible disclosure of crime that would make the edifice of public order reel, and startle us into such thoughtful anxiety as would unite us in the one great work of rooting out the vice, elevating the morals, and establishing on surer foundations the fabric of the great Republic.

Our city is full of unconverted men and women. What are we to do with them? Let them remain strangers to God, and ignorant of the Gospels? Is that the voice of our piety? It is full of ignorance and vice; it is full of license and misery. The soil under our feet is sown thick with the seeds of future crime; the air above us is hot with inflammable elements. We see our peril; we see our duty. Here the power of Christianity is to be put to the test before the eyes of the whole world. My friends, we must form some organization, with force sufficient to meet the emergency. We must take the last element of risk out of the future. We must make this city, — which was the cradle of American Liberty, the birthplace of our Nationality, — from Beacon Hill to North Street, all Christian.

SERMON XII.

THE MORAL CONDITION OF BOSTON, AND HOW TO IMPROVE IT.

I HAD intended, friends, to present to you, in this the closing discourse of the series, such statistics and data in respect to the moral condition of our city as would give you all an intelligent and exact understanding of the matter, and let you know just where we stand. But after having devoted much time, and not a little labor, to the compilation of the needed material I had obtained, I found that I had collected subject-matter for a volume rather than for one discourse; and I was constrained to omit altogether the data and explanation to which I have referred, and to confine myself to a course of discussion and suggestion this evening which, although less satisfactory to a student of social science, may prove more pleasant and profitable to a popular assemblage. And even after having adopted this latter plan, I found it impossible to compress within the required limits of time what I wished to say; and I shall, therefore, from a fear of wearying your patience, omit in the delivery a portion of my discourse.

One thing must be borne in mind by those who would obtain data on which to base an intelligent judgment. It is this, Where and what is the source of crime in this city? Where are the springs which feed this prurient reservoir? Whence come those streams of evil supply which keep this marsh of iniquity ever full of impure waters, ever dense with miasmatic vapors, of which virtue no sooner breathes than it dies? Does it feed itself? Is it a depth beneath which there is a deeper depth of ever-rising foulness? Does crime generate crime and disease disease, as virtue promotes virtue and health health? My friends, facts do not allow us so to conclude. Crime kills itself. Its law is not the law of life, but the law of death. The tendency of excess is to cut off the supply which feeds it. Indulgence does not beget healthy, long-lived offspring. It is among the poor, the vicious, and the sensual that Death has his own way. There disease meets few checks; sanitary precautions are unknown, unpractised, impossible. Left to the force and operation of its own laws of life and association, North Street would soon be depopulated. Scarce a babe born there would survive its infancy. Ere its young eyes had fully opened to the light they would be closed forever, and its little body would sleep in that silent chamber which is beyond the reach of neglect and cruelty.

No, the source of crime is not in North Street;

it lies farther up. There you behold the result, not the beginning; there are the bitter dregs, but if you would see the beaded surface of the cup you must look higher. Crime works downward. Like frost, it strikes the upper branches first. The dance-house and brothel are the last result of a long course of sinful indulgence. The wine-cup, the theatre, the ball-room, seduction, fashionable looseness in morals in the upper circles of society, — these are the sources whence flow those evil waters which, gathering impurity as they descend, stagnate at last in North Street.

In this connection you see the powerlessness of police regulations to reform society. Even if reformation ever came from repression, it would still be beyond the power of force to accomplish the desired end, because the seeds and roots of the evil are where the fingers of no municipal regulation can reach them. You cannot put espionage upon vice previous to some overt act. You can, it is true, station your police in the hovels and dance-houses of North Street, for there vice is open, coarse, uncovered; but you cannot enter the mansions of the rich, and those whose social position protects them from legal inquisition, — where vice, if it exist, is veiled under the gauze of outward propriety or rouged with the colors of virtue. This fact must ever be borne in mind by students of the social question.

But, in point of fact, force is not the agent of reformation. Correct morals cannot be beaten into a man by the *baton* of a policeman. The municipal court and the house of correction are not the fountains whence the waters of regeneration flow. Law can punish and kill, but it cannot redeem. It can confine the body, but it cannot renew the character. You may load down your statute-books with penal enactments until they cover every detail of crime, and yet not a thief would be made honest, not a fallen woman restored by your legislation. I know well that law can remove temptation from men; that it can check, by the fear of penalty, the open indulgence of existing passions; but farther than this we cannot rely on it. You must not suppose that when you have placed a policeman on every corner, and a detective in every dark alley, you have done all that you can do to improve the moral condition of your city, and make life and property safe. The tree whose every leaf represents a separate curse, whose odor is disease, and whose fruit is death, draws its life from soils far beneath the surface. Its roots are imbedded amid the ignorance, the appetites, and the passions of men. These law never reaches. You might as well expect to quiet the surging of a boiling caldron by skimming the surface as to quiet the evil agitations of men's hearts by legal enactments. In vain resort to law, in vain multiply police; the tumult will still go on, passions will still rage, appetites still seek indulgence, and the heart still beat behind the prison-bars with the same wild unrest that impelled to the commission of the crime. Law, therefore, — first, because it cannot reach the source of crime, and, secondly, because, if it could, it is unable to remove it, — cannot be relied upon to accomplish what is the crying necessity of the hour.

But if police regulations cannot effect the reformation, neither are the moral and spiritual forces now in the field able to accomplish the desired work. These forces may be represented by four elements of power, — the Church, the Mission School, the Public School, and the City Missionary Society. Take these in their order and examine them; observe the extent and the limitation of their power.

So far as the influence of the Church extends, it is potential for good. The preacher covers in his discourses a wide field of duty and instruction. There is little in ethics, there is little in politics, there is little in human progress, of which the pulpit does not treat. I am willing to grant all that the warmest advocate of the Church as a power in American society can claim. I appreciate fully the influence of repeated weekly ministrations of the clergymen of this city upon its morals and piety. So far as their voice extends, it is a voice of quickening and inspiration; but a vast multitude in this city never hear the preacher's voice. The glad news of redemption through Christ; the instruction which would, if heard, enlighten their minds; the exhortation which would strengthen their virtue; the supplication which would lift their hearts to the Throne, is never heard. The sound of no church-bell calls them to prayer; no altar invites their presence; no pastor watches over their souls. In a Christian land they are without Christianity; in a city of prayer their lips know not the habit or the value of supplication. Living by our very side, immortal as ourselves, they are without God and without hope in the world. Nor is there any prospect that this lamentable state of things will be changed for the better in the immediate future. The fashion of church architecture which is now in vogue is one of the most serious obstacles in the path of reform. Wealth builds the churches, not to accommodate the poor, but for wealth to worship in. I am not one of those who cry out against elaborate and costly edifices of worship. Let the architect and the artisan exhaust their utmost resources to adorn and make imposing the structures in which the Most High is to be adored. Nothing is too grand, vast, or magnificent for such a service. I only ask that, when erected, they shall be open

11*

to all. Let the wealthiest and the poorest, the strongest and the weakest, the taught and the untaught, worship side by side. But the day which shall see this aspiration realized in this country is, I fear, remote. Pride and fashion, prejudice and timidity, will be slow to yield their sovereignty over the American mind. The tide sets in the wrong direction, and the magnificent opportunity is floating away from us. As the facts now stand, our population is increasing much faster than our church accommodations; and he who looks to our churches to redeem our cities from their present deplorable state of semi-heathenism will live, I fear, to groan over a bitter disappointment.

The second agent which is now being relied upon to convert our cities is the Mission School.

My friends, I fear the position I must assume in this discourse will expose me to the charge of captiousness; but, believe me, I do not aspire to be regarded as a professional fault-finder. Neither in spirit nor in practice am I a carper. I only set myself to analyze certain factors which represent the present available moral forces of our city. If my analysis leads me to a conclusion other than hopeful, I am not to blame. I am guided, not by my desires, but by my convictions. I seek only the testimony of facts, and abide strictly by that decision which they compel. That mission schools accomplish much good, give much needed instruction, and in individual cases bring about a radical conversion, I do not deny. For years I served as a teacher or officer in them; for other years I have studied them and their influence in connection with my pastoral labors. I am an enthusiastic advocate of the system. But I am convinced that, though their influence for good is great, it is overrated by the public. The system is not capable of accomplishing any such results as are expected of it. Children that are depraved in private cannot be reformed in public. There is no influence that can stand against home influence. When the parents are as near being devils as the limitations of the flesh will allow, and home is a social and domestic hell; when the malevolent passions are the first to wake in the child's breast, and the first sounds its ears interpret are those of brawling and oaths; when all the surroundings of the boy are gross and sensual, his playmates incipient thieves, the hero of his neighborhood a successful burglar, and his vernacular the blasphemy which cuts the air like a flying scrap of red-hot iron, — it is like a farce to expect that an hour's instruction once a week in a mission school will reform him. That hour is like a plank thrust out from the bank into a seething current, but it is idle to suppose that it can hold its own for an instant against the one hundred and sixty-seven other hours of the week. The mission teacher has only one foot of the lever on his side, while the Devil has one hundred and sixty-seven on his, weighted also in his favor with natural and acquired depravity beyond estimate. Is there any doubt, friends, which will win, which will lift, the boy? Why, the Sabbath-school teacher has no chance at all! The odds are all against him. Now and then he makes a success. There are exceptions to every rule. I am not talking of these. I am not talking of what supernatural power may, at certain long intervals of time, effect. The age of miracles is not entirely passed. Now and then the voice, which even the grave must obey, speaks, and a soul, startled from a sleep heavier than that which held the body of Lazarus, comes forth to the amazement of its friends. But miracles are rare. We have no right to make them the basis of our expectations. And if we seriously propose to improve the moral condition of this city, we shall make a great mistake if we suppose that any multiplication of mission schools will do it. A city of debauched parents and godless homes will be a city of idiots and thieves and paupers until you reform these sources of their supply. Virtue, under certain conditions of life, is impossible: the conditions must be changed before it can exist. You might as reasonably expect to grow violets on Charles River flats as to rear a child in holiness in a basement in North Street. I have been in dens of this city where even a saint would stifle, so rank was the atmosphere with vice. The causes of crime do not lurk in the mind alone; they exist in the body as well. And the only way to reform the mind and soul is to reform the body first. Diet and cleanliness precede the Lord's Prayer in the alphabet of social ethics. One of the most practicable and worthy undertakings in the way of reform is, as it appears to me, the effort that is being made to provide Christian homes for the homeless children of our cities. This is better, so far as it is possible, than mission-school enterprises. There are thousands of children in this city to-night who can never become industrious and virtuous men and women here. They are like young and delicate plants which have sprung up in too damp a soil. They need transplanting. The gardener must go down into the soft muck, and run his fingers carefully under their roots, and set them in warmer and drier soil. So it is with these children. They are now in a moral marsh. All the conditions of growth are against them. We must lift them out of their present surroundings, and start them anew in better. Five thousand children should be sent into the country from Boston alone. The country wants them, and they need the air and work, and such homes as can be found nowhere save in the country. Take them from their debauched and brutalizing parents;

take them by the strong hand of legal provision, if necessary. You take them thus to send them to prison, the reform ship, and the house of correction ; can you not, then, take them in order to give them health and home and holiness ? Talk about parental rights ! What right has a father to brutalize his boy, to beat his body, to debase his soul, to educate him by speech and example to be a pauper, a thief, or a sot ? What right has a mother to prevent a girl's development in womanhood, to stand between her soul and virtue, between her mind and knowledge ? Has the State no rights in her children ? Is there a boy in your streets in whose growth and character the Commonwealth is not interested ? Has humanity no rights ? Are we to stand idly by, and see minds darkened and bodies diseased and souls *lost ?* Has God no rights, and must His people continue to see the city which religion founded and which religion has adorned surrendered over to a heathenism which has in it all the moral darkness of Africa, with a thousand-fold more cunning and viciousness ? Has Liberty no right even to protect herself ? Must she permit, without protest, the ark of her safety, the ballot-box, to be submerged and swamped beneath a rising deluge of vice and ignorance ? For one, I am not of the number who believe it. We have a right, I maintain, to take these children, by statute if need be, and put them a thousand miles from the corruption in which they had the misfortune to be born, — to place the width of the continent between them and that daily and hourly contamination which steals the name of mother and the title of father the better to fence itself from moral and legal check. Not only so, but it is the duty of the State to protect childhood from such influences as are sure, if allowed to exist, to prevent them from ever becoming honest, industrious, and intelligent citizens. The object of government is to preclude the need of jails and poor-houses, and not to build them, — to assist man to develop in worthy directions his character, and give the lowest a chance to rise. And, in the furtherance of this object, it has the right to separate the children of misfortune from the dire conditions of their birth, and remove them to more favorable ones of life and growth.

But it is not my intention to discuss all the minor questions of duty and expediency which grow out of the main consideration, — the moral improvement of our cities. I return from what may be regarded a digression to allude to one other movement in the right direction. I refer to what is known as the Industrial School enterprise.

Consider this matter a moment. Get an intelligent conception of the causes which make this movement eminently a necessity. There is a crime among us of which you all know by report at least, although I doubt if one in a hundred outside of the police force has any idea of the extent to which it abounds. And yet it seeks little concealment, — only enough to hide itself from the eyes of the unobserving, or those who do not wish to see. It walks your streets, infests your Common, rendezvouses in your theatres, rents your tenements, rustles its silks in some of your finest mansions,— even audiences convened for the worship of God have more than once been put under police espionage in this city to protect the sanctity of the occasion from the intrusion of this nameless crime. Now whence does it get its supply? Having in the lives of its personal victims but an average of three years, and losing thirty per cent of its number every twelve months, how comes it that its ranks are ever full? Through what conductors that impart poison come the waters that keep this polluted cistern filled continually to its very brim? Well, there are many sources of supply. Seduction yields a certain proportion; inherent depravity adds its per cent; intemperance and ill-treatment by parents, relatives, or husbands; indolence; evil companionship, — each yields its share to swell the awful tide: but another cause remains to be mentioned, which gives, according to the best data gathered, over one fourth of the whole number, — it is *destitution.* Of two thousand subjects examined in New York City, it was ascertained that five hundred and twenty-five were compelled to become prostitutes through destitution. They had no inclination for the horrid life; every instinct of their natures rebelled against it; but they were driven to it by sheer starvation. Mothers sold their chastity to buy bread for their children; daughters, to procure medicines for their sick parents, — yea, in some cases, that their mothers might have a roof to shelter them in their last sickness, and a bed on which to die in peace. This is not imagination employed to paint a picture to excite your sympathy; I am only quoting official facts and figures. Nor was this destitution, in the majority of cases, the result of improvidence; it was the natural result of that false system of female education which prevails in this country, which leaves the women of the land to the sport of a fickle fortune. We educate our girls to spend and not to earn, to depend upon others for support and not upon themselves, — leaving them at the same time exposed to every contingency of sickness and death, which often deprives them in a moment of that support which they need, and without which they cannot live with virtue, unless assisted by charity. I know that we plume ourselves upon the educational facilities that we enjoy. It is our boast that knowledge is open to all; and the boast is allowable, if by knowledge you mean only that which belongs to scholarship, which adorns character with the power and grace of intellectual acquisition, which fits our girls for the parlor and for that leisure and refined companionship which wealth and fashion secure and demand. But if knowledge means something more than this, — if it includes that power which enables one to support himself, which makes the fingers worthy allies of the brain, which arms one against the contingencies of life, the uncertainties of fortune, — if knowledge means this, — then is our boast but the assumption of unthinking conceit, for such knowledge America does not give and never has given to her children.

Why, look at your educational system. Examine it soberly a moment, and see what it does and does not do.

You take a girl of poor parentage and social inferiority, whose parents do not know perhaps how to read or write, yet a girl of promise, quick to learn, apt to imitate, physically beautiful. For eight years — years which cover the formative period of her life — you give her the best advantages of your superb public schools. She sits at the same desk with the rich man's daughters, recites in the same class, studies the same books, hears their conversation, adopts their standard of taste, their ideas of dress and views of life and labor.

For eight years you have been educating her to love ease and refinement, and all the concomitants of such a state. At last the girl is graduated, — graduated, I will admit, a lady. You have taught her art and science, literature and poetry, made her fit for the parlor and the mansion. You have educated her pride, her vanity, her taste. You have unfitted her for her former life and sphere. Will she go down and drudge with her ignorant mother? Will she mate with and marry the companion of her coarse, hard-working brothers? My friends, such a supposition is against all reason. It flies in the face of well-established social tendencies. No, you have made her a lady, as Americans understand that term, and a lady she will be. If her beauty and accomplishments win her a husband able to provide her with a home, that home she will adorn and that husband she will make happy. If not, *what?* Will some of you answer? You have made her a queen, now guarantee her a throne. What can she do? Teach, you say. Fifty applicants for every position, I respond. She might set type, and earn from twelve to twenty dollars per week; but you have not taught her. She might operate a telegraph, but she knows not even the alphabet of the art. She might mould and engrave, and win a generous support, perhaps fame; but your schools provide no teachers for so beautiful and lucrative a profession. She might even earn a fair competence as a seamstress, but the whirr of a sewing-machine would disturb the class in philosophy and French. What can she do, I repeat? Clerk it for six dollars per week, and pay five for her board and room-rent!

My friends, virtue will not live at such a rate. You have no right to expect it will. If you educate girls to expect luxury, you must provide them with the means to honestly obtain it. It is the duty of those who shape society to remove temptation from the people, to make virtue easy, and put vice at the greatest possible disadvantage. But the educational and social system which we tolerate in America reverses this wise rule. We make vice easy, nay, almost a necessity, in that we educate our girls for a style of life which nothing but labor liberally compensated, or vice, can support, and then deny them both the labor and the compensation. Under the workings of our present arrangements virtue starves and vice feasts. The one drudges its life out in rags; the other promenades your streets in silks. Many a female clerk can save but a dollar a week. That is the amount she has left after deducting the cost of her board and lodging. The pitiful sum represents six days of weary toil. But a smile will buy her a dress, and a week's compliance with temptation put more money in her pocket than she could save by the practice of a year's economy. Such are the facts of the case, and the crime will increase so long as the cause is allowed to remain.

If an enlarged system of education be objected to on the ground of expense; if you should say, "Your theory is correct enough, but its reduction to practice would add twenty per cent to the cost of maintaining our public schools, and we cannot afford it," I reply, You can afford anything which lessens crime twenty per cent. Virtue is never dear and vice never cheap at any price. Contented and hopeful Industry, and Morality, her twin-sister, — these are to the state what springs are to rivers; and whatever can add appreciably to these should receive at once the attention and support, not only of those in authority, but of all who have the honor of the Commonwealth and the good of humanity at heart.

I have now spoken of the Church, the Mission School, and the Common School as agents of reform, and suggested the weakness, the limitations, and the inefficiency of each, as measured by the especial work to be done. Only one more agent remains to be considered. I refer to those efforts which for the most part are made through what are known as City Missionary Societies.

These societies accomplish, beyond doubt, much good. The persons employed are men and women of piety and zeal. Far be it from me to lessen in the least the value of their self-denying labors, or detract an iota from the estimation in which they are deservedly held by the Christian public. I am not talking of persons, but of systems; not of agents, but of organizations. Speaking thus, and with no personal allusions whatever, I maintain that city missionary societies are doing, and can do, as now conducted, scarcely anything to meet the physical and moral necessities of our city. Individuals here and there are assisted, — fed, clothed, and reformed; but the ignorant, impoverished, and vicious class, as a *class*, remains substantially untouched. There are many reasons to account for this state of things. In the first place, we have not admitted our responsibility in the matter. The Christian public have not seriously interested themselves in it. We have not confessed, even to ourselves, that we are under any obligation to the poor, the fallen, and the falling; our aim, our chief effort, has been to protect ourselves from them. If we could keep our lives and property passably safe; if, through police regulations, we could overawe the vicious classes, and keep them in subjection to law, so that they should not gain the ascendency and imperil our material interests; if we could only confine them within certain sections of the city, as we do Indians upon their reservations, we have been content. But that we were really responsible before God for their moral condition, or had any positive obligation in the matter, this we have never seriously believed.

In the second place, we have never made any downright, determined effort to overcome the evil. It has been fashionable for each of our churches to sustain a mission school, to support a city missionary, and take up occasionally a contribution for the "Wanderers' Home," and similar institutions, and so we have done it; but as to joining hands in fraternal union, as to rising in our might and saying, "Cost what it may, this shame and danger must be removed from our midst, this home heathenism must be rooted out," we never have done it. No such effort has been made here as was made under the leadership of Chalmers in Edinburgh to reform the vicious classes of that city. We have worshipped our God in comfortable temples, sung our hymns of praise and joy, indulged in splendid seclusion our hopes of heaven, as if there were not thousands within the sound of our Sabbath chimes who had no temples in which to worship, no hymns to sing, no joy to cherish. And if we have at intervals warmed up to the work of saving souls, if we have longed and given to spread the Gospel news, it has been for the Caffre and the benighted heathen on some far-distant shore, and not for men and women living and dying at our very side, who know nothing of Jesus save as a term with which to edge their wit or emphasize an oath. And if one, driven by curiosity or some worthier motive, goes down into this moral Gehenna that yawns at our very feet, and, returning therefrom as from the very valley of corruption, lifts his voice to tell us of the sights he saw and the sounds he heard, we regard him as a second-rate sensationalist, whose trade it is to deal out to his audiences exaggerated descriptions of pathetic and horrible experiences. The speaker is not credited, and the audience remains unconvinced.

The best plan, as it appears to me (to get at the matter in a business-like way) is to do here what Chalmers did in Edinburgh, — district the city, and apportion the districts among those churches of the city willing to embark in the enterprise. Hold each church responsible for its section, and let none undertake to cover more territory than can be cultivated thoroughly, *and at once.* The work should include every branch of reformation, beginning with the lowest, and in certain sections of our city it would be found to be the most essential, — the body. Cleanliness precedes piety in the order of spiritual development. The bath-tub before the Bible, soap before the religious tract. The work must be from house to house, one at a time, and, as the prime condition of success, in connection with *civil authority and co-operation with the police.*

This last suggestion may appear startling to you. It certainly is novel, but I am convinced that it is both necessary and feasible. Indeed, I would not predict success of the most earnest effort, under the most judicious management, on any other condition. In order that any salutary reform may be effected, certain nuisances must be abated, which can be done only through civil action. Certain laws, now a dead letter or nearly so, must be rigidly enforced, but this can be done only through the police department. The moral and the civil forces must work in union in order to effect their object. At present they are divorced, and alone neither can accomplish what they might if united.

Look at this matter a moment. The first essential of reform is knowledge. The reformer must make himself acquainted with the habits and customs of the depraved, and the causes which lead them astray, and which now operate to keep them in bondage. He must learn to distinguish between the hardened criminal and the novice in crime, and tell at a glance to which class a person belongs. He must know the haunts of vice, the dens of infamy, the hovels of poverty, and all the concomitants of those whom he is to benefit. Without such knowledge he is as powerless to help as a physician, when he finds himself face to face with a new, unheard-of, and virulent form of contagion. Well, what do we do? Why, we elect some pious woman as our city missionary, — a woman who knows no more of vice in its origin, growth, subterfuges, and deceits than your wife by your side, my friend. You send out that woman, fitted neither by nature nor education for the work, and pit her against the hardest, most cunning, shrewdest class of our population. They masquerade to her face, and laugh at her behind her back. She is a mere shuttle for the nervous strokes of their wit to pass to and fro between the warp of their coarse mirth. You have sent her to a work novel, arduous, demanding peculiar natural qualities and a peculiar knowledge which she does not possess, and the result is what every intelligent person would expect: the ignorant are ignorant still, and the tide of vice and evil indulgence casts its sluggish waters higher and higher up, until they wash the very foundations of your churches. I would give more for two Christian ex-policemen as city missionaries than any fifty church-members you may select and send down as evangelists to North Street. My two would relieve more honest poverty, stop more brutality, minister to more sickness, reform more drunkards, lift more of the fallen, detect more hypocrisy, do more good, than all your fifty put together.

And here permit me to say a word concerning the *personnel* of your police force. For a year I have watched the department closely, made myself acquainted with the duties and responsibilities of the policeman, as he goes his daily and nightly rounds. I know the estimation in which the average policeman is held by the wicked, the poor, and the unfortunate; and here I bear a sincere and, as I believe, an intelligent testimony, not merely as to faithfulness in discharge of their difficult duties, but more especially in reference to their character and standing as men, amid the classes with which they are more immediately brought in contact. Of their official conduct and services public reports speak; but of their numberless acts of kindness to the poor, their deeds of charity to the friendless, their self-sacrifice, often of both time and money, to assist the destitute and the unfortunate,—of these it is in my power, as it is certainly a pleasure for me, to bear witness. Many a warm Christian heart beats under the policeman's badge. Many a patrolman of your city has endeared himself to the poor and the sick of his beat by his deeds of love and his words of counsel and sympathy. More than one member of the force, as I have reason to know, has fulfilled the highest ideal of a police-officer, in that he is regarded, not merely as an officer of the law, but as a friend and counsellor in times of trouble. My warmest sympathy and admiration are given to these men, who, without the support or praise of any, without even any profession on their part, are doing noble missionary service for the city and for God.

My idea is, as I have said, that all our missionary efforts should be conducted in connection with the civil power and the police. We need the knowledge that these men alone can give us. What do we clergymen and citizens know of the unfortunate and criminal classes of our city, compared with these men whose duty it is to become intimately acquainted with them? They have studied the problem as we have not. Standing amid the results of indulgence and crime, they can tell you the causes, point out the several stages of that long yet swift descent which, beginning at the level of innocence, landed the girl in North Street. Take any clergyman in this city; let him doff his clerical robes and don the blue uniform, and pass five years on his beat in North Street, — every day and night of those years on the alert, studying countenances, watching modes of life and their results, seeing the benefit and the abuse of law, learning the goodness and the meanness of men as only a patrolman can, — studying this great problem of the causes which vitiate a population, and which reform. Let a clergyman do this for five years, I say, and what professional brother in this city would be able to advise, touching missionary work, as could he? But if five years could do so much to furnish one with needed knowledge for this service, what must we conclude concerning those who have spent ten, fifteen years, nay, almost a lifetime, as some of your police-officers have, in just this business? If I had the missionary work of this city intrusted to me to organize and conduct, the first thing I should do would be to invite the Mayor of the city and the captains of the police to assist me in mapping out the plan, and urge their co-operation in its general execution. More intelligent, willing, and zealous co-laborers it would be difficult to find. I am not sure but that, before this great work will ever be intelligently undertaken, some central organization must be formed; a church dedicated solely for this purpose must be built, open to all willing to work for God and man, — a church of great wealth, gathered from all denominations, and numerous in membership, manifold in diversity of talents, whose sole mission shall be to wash and whiten the moral uncleanliness of Boston. All hail to the day when such a church shall take its stand among us, and proclaim, "For the sake of the Republic, for the sake of humanity, and — nobler motive yet — for the glory of God, we devote the energies, the prayers, the wealth of this church, to the Christianization of Boston."

My friends, I thank you for your patience, which I feel I have sorely taxed to-night, and for the courtesy and kindness with which you have here received my words. I will detain you but a moment longer. It is to say that, upon whatever sanitary and reformative agents we may rely to assist us in the work, it is in religion alone that we can find the motives and the spirit needed. It is the power of God unto salvation that we must have with us in all our efforts, if we are to succeed. Not to the body alone does triumph come through the Cross, but a more far-reaching and extensive victory comes to the soul. The soul has its diseases, — where shall it find a physician? It is stricken with weakness, — by whom shall it be braced with power? There is to virtue a grave, and the wailing above it is sadder than the surge of winds through the cypress. Hot are the tears that fall above it, and no human cry can express the agony of a spirit bowed down in despair, and groaning for virtue lost, for manhood smitten, for honor gone forever. Show me where love was lost, where faith was rent, where hope died out, where all that made the man went down, and I will show you a spot too sad for cypress, too black for crape; and yet hope may come to that despondent soul and light to that darkened spot.

Nevermore shall the stricken eagle rise; nevermore with living wing shall it sport along the edges of the tempest and rise superior to the cloud; never will the Sun behold it in its aspiring flight, and take it to himself, hiding it from mortal sight in the blaze of his brightness; but, lifeless and debased, it shall lie until the worm shall know it, and the vile things that crawl feed on the plumage of the sky.

But to the stricken soul, to the debased spirit, to overthrown manhood there is a hope. The Gospel speaks, and that which had no power to rise is lifted. Life comes back to it. Strength throbbing with power; vigor which beats with full vein; aspirations which outsoar the eagle's flight, leaving the sun beneath them; hope that contents itself with nothing that is not heaven; and a purpose which bears the buffets of evil fortune without a murmur, which keeps an even pace against a tornado's pressure, — all these come to the soul through Christ, renewing the marred features until the original loveliness appears, as tints in colored marble grow under the smoothing-plane, and man resumes once more the long-lost look of God. O men and women without the power of the Gospels in your hearts, how much you lose! Give up your wealth; fling beauty aside, yea, fling it from you until you shall be as was the Man of Sorrows, in whom men saw no comeliness; part with position and all that vanity craves; — only have the power of God's transforming love in your hearts, and your wealth shall be beyond the riches of men. and your royalty beyond the royalty of kings.

People talk about religion being a restraint upon men. And so it is in one sense,—but it is a very small sense indeed. There are in man certain destructive tendencies,—passions which make him their sport, appetites which coerce his better judgment,—and religion puts a curb upon these and reins them in. But religion has other and larger uses than this. Fetters and cords and gags do not represent it. It directs more than it dams up; it germinates more than it stamps out. God purifies the soul very much as you air your rooms. You do not keep the doors and windows shut, and throw in chemicals, trusting that they will master and renew the vitiated element; you open all the doors and windows and ventilators, and let God's pure air flow in from without,—a strong, crisp current through every door and window, and thus you purify your chambers. So it is with God. The purifying influences come from without, not from within. He throws open all the windows of the soul,—the windows of feeling, of impulse, of imagination, of purpose,—and sends a strong current of vitalizing grace sweeping through them, until every apartment of our nature is reoxygenized and made healthy and bracing. Negatives do not express religious duty. The "shall nots" are less frequent than the "shalls." I love to think that religious life is the growth of all the faculties, and not a slow strangulation of them. As I look at it, religion no more cramps a man than wings do a bird or fins do a fish. It supplies him with propelling power. A Christian man should be an active man, — active in every faculty, every fibre vibrating with energy. Great injury has been done religion by allowing people to regard it as a mild form of slavery, a kind of bondage to goodness, in which people consented to be tied up that they might not hurt themselves or others. But there is no such religion as this, — at least in the New Testament. The Gospel Christ taught and Paul preached is a gospel of liberty and not of slavery. The more that faith in Christ works out its legitimate effect in man, the more is he emancipated, the freer he becomes. You all see this. You can each of you recall, probably, some person in slavery to some particular form of sin, — some habit, some appetite. Take the appetite for alcoholic liquor. Let it once get its fingers fairly around a man's throat, and it rarely lets go until it flings him aside as a corpse. When the man is black in the face, and his blood chilled forever, and his body fit only for the worm, then it quits its hold, but rarely before. While he lives the man is the slave of his sinful habit. To it he gives his earnings, his time, his health, the clothes on his back, even his children's bread, — all go to gratify the cravings of his appetite. But let the grace of God come into his soul, and his fetters are broken; he stands disenthralled and erect, a free man.

I tell you, friends, there is hope for all. Christ is able to save even unto the uttermost. Only make the Gospels known, only preach them so that men can understand them, only keep this radiant sun in the heavens, and the spiritual nature of men must blossom. You might as well charge the swelling buds in June not to open and grow fragrant when the beams of the sun are prying open all their leaves, and the south-wind is forcing itself in among the petals, as to forbid men to flower out in goodness under the influence of the Gospels.

I preach the message of God to you, therefore, not with threats. I tilt against your fears with no spear-like denunciation. The message I am set to carry to my fellow-men is not one of terror, but of glad news. I know that God is inflexible in justice toward those who persist in wickedness. I know that His wrath, when kindled, can burn to the lowest hell; but fear is not a gospel motive, terror is not a substitute for love. He does not drive men, He guides. He does not threaten, He invites. Christ did not come to condemn the world, but that the world through Him might be saved. This has been greatly overlooked. The

New Testament has often been preached as a book of legislation rather than of salvation. Christ has been held up as one who is to judge the world rather than one who is to save the world. This is a horrible perversion of His mission. I present God to you, this evening, not in His judicial but His paternal relations to men. You are all His children; erring and disobedient some of you, but children still. His heart is full of love for you. His face is not averted in anger. He lifts the light of it upon you at this moment. Some of you, perhaps, are discouraged. He says, "My child, be of good courage, I am with you always." Some of you are weak and weary; you have walked far and borne much. He says, "My child, see, thou art weak, but I am strong; thou art small, but I am vast; come to my arms, lay yourself on my bosom, and I will carry you the rest of the way." Some of you are in grief; the voices of the departed are ever in your ears, their faces ever before your eyes; you cannot at times eat or sleep because of your weeping. "Hush," He says, "subdue your grief, and live your days in hope and joy. Heaven is large, and its ministrations are abundant. The departed are with me; when you meet them again, you shall have them forever." And some of you are far off, rebellious and bitter. But does He pursue you in wrath, does He smite you? Ah *no;* the rain falls on the just and the unjust. He calls to you, He sends me as His messenger out after you, with the command, "Tell them to come back, yea, every one. I would not that any should perish. Tell them all to come back to their Father's love and home." Let this be the closing utterance, the last words, probably, which, as a preacher of the Gospel, I shall ever address to you from this platform. In weariness and weakness often, amid doubts of purpose and of plan, in narrowness of conception, in feebleness of expression, I have striven for these twelve nights to teach and inspire, to direct and encourage you. Through them all God has been with us on our right hand and on our left; and at times I have seen, or thought I saw, among us the Presence which is ineffable.

Believing most firmly in the power of the Gospel to save, in the efficacy of the Blood to atone, in the willingness of God to forgive, in His love for the lowly and the lost, I launch this voice into the air; I send it out over the city — would that it might reach every heart and every ear! — "Come back, all ye who have wandered from virtue, — come back to your Father's love and home."

THE END.

Cambridge: Electrotyped by Welch, Bigelow, & Co.

www.ingramcontent.com/pod-product-compliance
Lightning Source LLC
LaVergne TN
LVHW010229110826
845151LV00004B/1235

9781425526481